to MacOS Big Sur

All You Need to Know to be a Professional User of the MacOS Big Sur on MacBooks and iMacs

ROBERT KISSINGER

Copyright

Printed on acid-free paper.

Table of Contents

CHAPTER ONE

What is new in the macOS Big Sur

Apple announced the macOS Big Sur in the June 2020 WWDC. The macOS Big Sur is the latest mac operating system, which is the macOS 11. The macOS 11 was later released November 12, 2020. The macOS Big Sur, which was un-boxed with the latest mac features, has been the talk of Apple enthusiasts across the world.

The following are the important features and updates in the macOS 11;

- **Lighter window look:** Windows now come with a lighter and more sizable look making them cleaner and very easy to work with. Also noticeable is the incorporated translucency and rounded edges that were designed to give mac a nice feel and look.

- To get more attention on contents, the app's **controls and buttons** now show when you need them and then disappear when you are not using them. In addition, there is a **customized menu bar** which gives you access to a **customized Control Center.** The customized control center is the one that contains **Bluetooth, Dark Mode, Do Not Disturb, Keyboard brightness, sound level, AirDrop controls etc**.

- The Notification Center now comes with added **interactive notifications** that have been grouped by app. There is also the inclusion of **iOS-style widgets** customizable in three different sizes. For easy interaction with your apps, there is an updated arrangement for core applications, which gives improved organization for many open windows.
- Safari, more than ever before, is now faster and battery efficient and also contains a new start page customizable with wallpapers of choice. There are also sections such as **iCloud Tabs** and **Reading List.** It is now easier to find

app extensions, and there is now an additional feature that will allow you to move extensions from Firefox and Chrome browser easily to Safari. In addition, **tabs** have also been redesigned (displaying more tabs on the screen) to allow you navigate Safari faster and efficiently. Now, users can decide which websites can use Safari extension and when the website can use it.

- There are now some good improvements in Safari privacy with a **Privacy Report** allowing users to see which trackers Safari has blocked anytime you visit websites. Also, Safari now comes with a **built-in translation** option enabling users to translate a whole page of a website in seven different languages just with a single click.

Password: Apple now uses **password monitoring** to inform users of any data breach for passwords that are saved in the iCloud Keychain. The **password monitoring** is a protection feature that generates strong passwords automatically to enforce more security.

Messages: The messaging system in the macOS Big Sur now uses the same features as the **Messages app** in the iOS 14, which include many features like the **inline replies, @mentions, pinned conversations etc.** Now, you can use Messages effects just the way it is in iOS with supported features like **Memoji stickers** and **Memoji creation.** In addition, there is a total overhauling in the manner searches are being conducted in the **Messages app;** this makes it especially very easy to find photos, matching terms and links. Also, there is a new photo picker which allows you to easily find pictures using keywords and you can then send them to families and friends. The photo picker also comes with trending GIFs and images, which you can add to your message.

The **Maps** app was not left behind as there is now better support for **Guides, indoor maps** and **Look Around** which all provide a list of notable restaurants and attraction centers. You can use the Maps for macOS to **generate cycling and electric vehicle trips**, which you can, sent to iPhone, and you can now access **shared ETA updates** on the mac.

There is now extended editing functionality in the **Photos app** having a new **Retouch tool** that is being run by machine learning. Also, **Apple Music** has been totally over-hauled with a "Listen Now" section containing personalized playlists, artist interviews and new releases.

Looking at the **Home app,** the **HomeKit Secure Video cameras** now has improved support for **Activity Zones** and **Face Recognition**, **AirPods** now have improved (better than it was before) **automatic device switching**, and Siri, now, can answer a much wider question range than it can in the past macOS updates.

In addition, Apple has speculated that the apps in the **mac App Store** would, in the future, aid users to better understand information collected by app developers before any user gets to download their apps, and also the privacy practices. Apple has correlated this feature with a food nutrition label for the apps in the App Store for mac.

macOS Big Sur brings **faster updates** which begin from the background and end rather quickly making it especially very easy to update your mac. Also, there is a **cryptographically signed system volume** protecting your gadget against tampering.
Some other features are;

- History of how you used your battery for the past ten days.

- Apps with subscription now have family sharing support.

- Notes app comes with improved search and quick editing

- You can also add reminders to individuals with the Reminders app

- There is an enhanced performance for spotlight
- Weather reports, including minute-by-minute precipitation reports in the Weather app.

Who should not install the macOS Big Sur for now?

Individuals using the 13 inch MacBook Pro models produced in late 2013 and mid 2014 should not install the macOS Big Sur at the moment. This is because there is a case of reported **bickering** in these machines. Across Apple communities and some forums on Reddit, users with these machines (13 inch MacBook Pro models produced in the late 2013 and mid 2014) are complaining that their gadgets are stuck with black screen while updating to the macOS Big Sur. Some combinations of key resets like the internet recovery, safe mode, NVRAM and SMC have been reported not to be working properly while attempting to install the macOS Big Sur.

There is hope that Apple will fix these issues in times to come. But other MacBook users can go ahead and install the macOS Big Sur on their mac.

Installing the macOS Big Sur on your mac

The file size for the latest macOS is about 12GB, hence you must have about 16GB storage in order to fully download the update. You also need to be patient as it might take time before the download is completed. To download the update on your mac, follow the steps below;

- **Check if your version of mac is actually compatible with the macOS Big Sur**. For convenience, the following devices are compatible with the latest macOS Big Sur; MacBook released in 2015 or later, MacBook Air released in

2013 or later, MacBook Pro released in the late 2013 and later, Mac mini released in 2014 and later, iMac released in 2014 and later, iMac Pro, and the Mac Pro from 2013 or later.

- **Create a backup for your mac:** The backup is necessary in case you encounter a problem along the line and you want to restore your contents or downgrade the operating system. Follow the steps below to properly backup your mac using **Time Machine** – which is the in-built backup feature on your mac computer;

How to create a Time Machine backup

You will need an external storage to start backing up your files with Time machine. Files like apps, music, videos etc can usually be backed up on your mac. To begin, simply connect the external storage device and choose the external storage as the backup disk on your mac computer. The Time machine will start to provide hourly backup in the last 24 hours, daily backup for the past months, and your weekly backup for all of the previous months. Once the backup disk is full, the oldest backups are automatically deleted.

How to connect the external storage device to your mac

The external storage devices below can be connected to your mac;

- A USB or Thunderbolt external drive connected to your Mac.
- A Network-attached storage (NAS) gadget which can support Time Machine over SMB
- Another Mac that has been shared as a destination of the Time Machine backup.
- An AirPort Time Capsule, or an external drive that has been connected to an AirPort Time capsule or AirPort Extreme Base Station (802.11ac)

Note: These external storage devices are usually sold separately and won't necessarily come with your mac on purchase.

Choose your storage device as the backup disk

1. Launch the **Time Machine preferences** right from the **Time Machine menu** from the menu bar. Or you can alternatively select Apple menu , click on **System Preferences**, and then tap "**Time Machine**.'
2. Tap on "**Select Backup Disk.**"

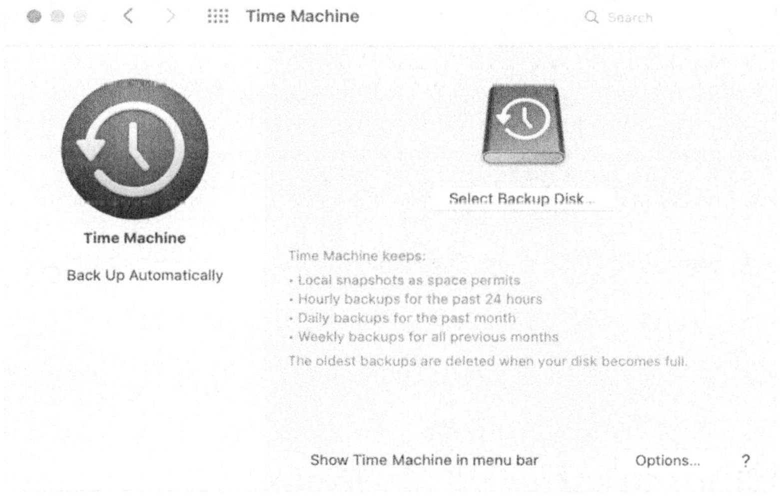

3. You will be shown the list of backups that are available, simply choose your own

backup disk. You can also make your account accessible to only those who have the backup password; you can just choose "Encrypt backups". Then tap on "Use Disk" found at the bottom right.

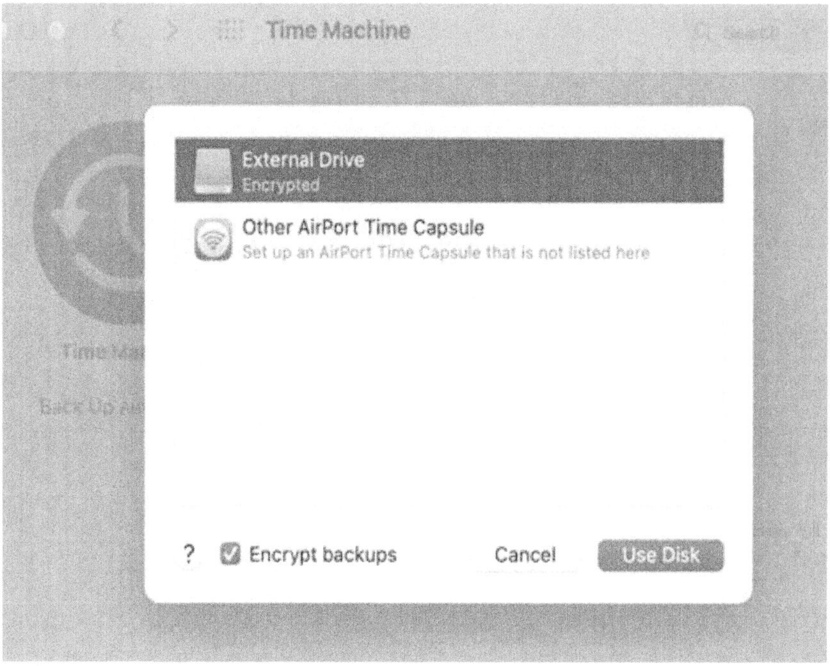

You can be asked to firstly erase the disk if the disk you chose has not been properly formatted to the specification of the Time Machine. Simply tap on "Erase" to continue. This action will delete all the information on that particular backup disk.

How to carry out an automatic backup

After you have chosen your desired backup disk, the Time Machine will immediately start to make periodic back-ups—without you necessarily initiating it. Usually, the first backup will take a much longer time than the subsequent ones; although you can still use the mac even while the backup is ongoing. To save time, the Time Machine will only back up those files that changed since the last time you carried out a backup on your mac.

If you wish to begin a manual backup, simply select "Back Up Now" from the menu of the Time Machine in the menu bar. The same menu can still be used to check your backup status or to skip a backup process.

- Once you have successfully created a backup, you need to make sure you have secured internet access, as the download will be done over the internet.
- **Download the macOS Big Sur:** For those using the former macOS Mojave, they can always install the macOS Big

Sur via a software update by simply clicking on **Apple Menu** , followed by **System Preferences** and then tap on **Software update.** And for those who want to get the latest update on the mac App Store, they can follow the link https://apps.apple.com/us/app/macos-bigsur/id1526878132?ls=1&mt=12 and then tap on the blue **Get button** or the **iCloud icon** to download the update.

- Once the file has been downloaded successfully, the installer will be opened automatically where you can tap on **continue** and then follow necessary instructions that will be shown on the screen.

- Let the file install completely and don't close the lid of your mac or put your mac in sleep mode.

Can't install macOS Big Sur?

The macOS Big Sur has become a big addition to the macOS lines since its release on November 12, 2020. Notwithstanding, some users have been reporting that they are unable to install the latest macOS update on their mac. These users have been found to be users who are using the old MacBooks (especially those released in 2013 and mid 2014). They reported that their MacBook refused to turn on or the update has refused to work at all after installing the update. If you are experiencing this problem, here are tips you can consider to get pass this limitation;

- Press and then hold on the power button of your Mac for about10 seconds, then release the power button. This turns off your mac.
- Proceed by unplugging any external gadget you have attached to your mac, and

you should also remove any card you have inserted in the mac's SDXC card slot, and then turn on your Mac.

- If the problem still persists, you can reset the SMC by;
    - Putting Off your Mac.
    - Press and then hold all of these keys on your built-in keyboard; **Shift** ⇧ key located to the left side of the keyboard; **Control** ^ located to the left of the keyboard and **Option** (Alt) ⌥ located to the left of the keyboard
    - While you are still holding **all of the three keys** described above, quickly press and then hold your mac's **power button** also.
    - Maintain the holding position for all of the four keys for about 10 seconds.
    - Release all of the keys, and then press your mac's **power button** to turn the mac on.

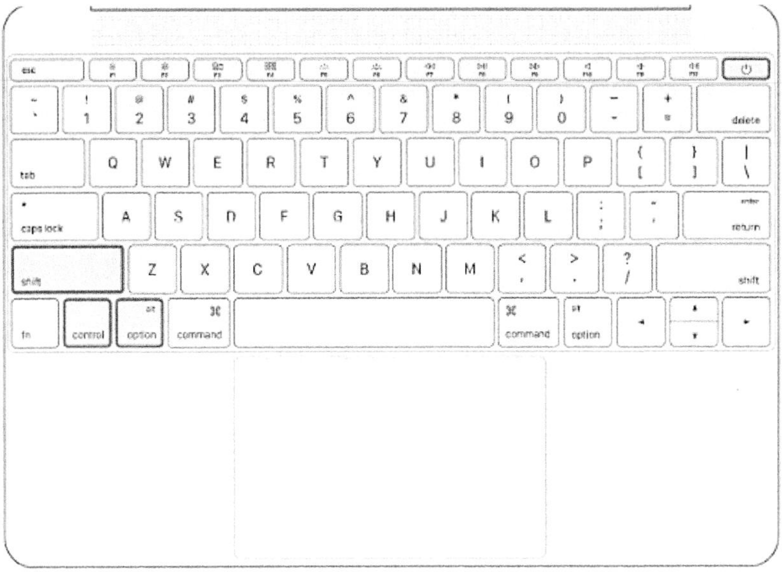
esc
~ ` ! 1 @ 2 # 3 $ 4 % 5 ^ 6 & 7 * 8 (9) 0 _ - + = delete
tab Q W E R T Y U I O P { [}] | \
caps lock A S D F G H J K L : ; " ' enter return
shift Z X C V B N M < , > . ? / shift
fn control option command command option

CHAPTER TWO

THE mac DESKTOP

The Menu Bar: what is it?

You will see the menu bar running along the top of the mac screen. The menu bar contains icons and menus where you can choose commands to execute, check status and perform some tasks.

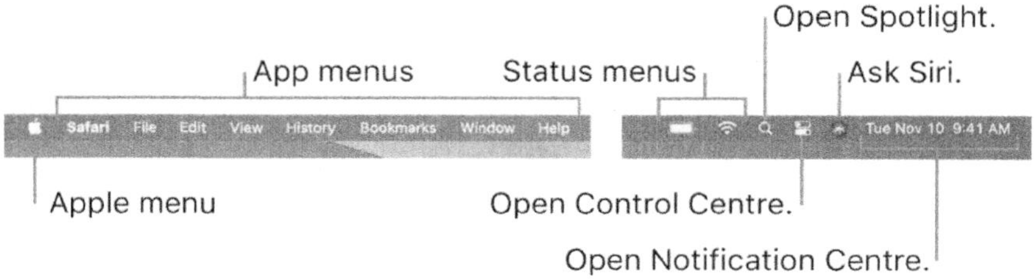

You can always hide your menu bar automatically so that it is only displayed anytime the pointer is moved to the top side of the screen. To do this, click on the Apple menu , select **System Preferences**, and then click on the "Dock & Menu Bar" where you can choose which feature to show or hide.

Apple menu

Check the top left side of your screen for the Apple menu . It is in fact the first item you see at the top. The Apple Menu contains commands for actions you do on your mac most frequently, like lock screen, shut down mac, open your system preferences or update your apps.

App menus

Just beside the Apple Menu is the App menu. The app you are currently using will show in the App menu with the name in bold, followed by some other menus with standard names like Window, Edit, File. Each of your apps will have a Help menu, which makes it very easy to get information about the app.

Each menu has commands, which are as well an essential feature of most apps. For instance, you will often see the open command inside the File menu.

Status menus

The **status menus are found to the right side of the menu bar, and are** always represented with icons, which enable you to view the status of your computer, or to even help you customize some features like the keyboard brightness.

To access more options or details, simply tap on a status menu icon. For instance, click on Wi-Fi to view the list of available networks, or tap Display to turn on/off Dark Mode or Night Shift. on or off.

You can rearrange the status menu by pressing and holding the command key as you drag an icon. You can, on the other hand, remove or delete a status menu by pressing and holding the Command key as you drag the icon you want to remove out of the status bar.

Spotlight

If you can see the Spotlight icon on the menu bar, tap on the icon so that you will be able to look for things on the web and on your Mac.

Control Center

Launch the Control Center by clicking on the Control Center icon . The Control Center will allow you access to some features that you used most frequently like the **AirDrop, Do Not Disturb** feature, **AirPlay** etc.

Siri

If you can see the Siri icon from the menu bar, tap on the icon to request Siri to do things for you. Siri can open apps, files and can even find things for you on your mac or from the internet.

Notification Center

Located at the right side of the menu bar is where you can click on the date and time to launch the Notification Center. The Notification Center is where you will be able to view your appointments, weather, notes and see notifications you have missed.

Using Spotlight to search on Mac

With Spotlight, you can easily locate apps, files and some other document type on your Mac. The **Siri suggestion** can also help you with sports score, weather highlights, latest news and lots more. You can also do some simple and basic calculation with the Spotlight feature.

Use Siri. You can request something like "How many grams make one kilogram" or ask "what is the value of pi?

Searching for something?

1. From your Mac, tap on the Spotlight icon (if you can see it) found in the menu bar or press the Command-Space bar or click on (if you can see it from the functions on your keyboard.

   The spotlight window can also be dragged anywhere you wish on the mac desktop. If you are unable to see the Spotlight window on the menu bar, you can add it by clicking on the Apple menu , select **System Preferences**, and then click on the "Dock & Menu Bar" where you can choose which feature to show .

2. Enter the name of the item you want to find inside the search field, and you will see the result appearing as you type.

   The Spotlight will first list top hits for you; tap on a top hit if you wish to preview it or if you just want to open it. The Spotlight will also suggest various search result and you can always select the one you want to see.

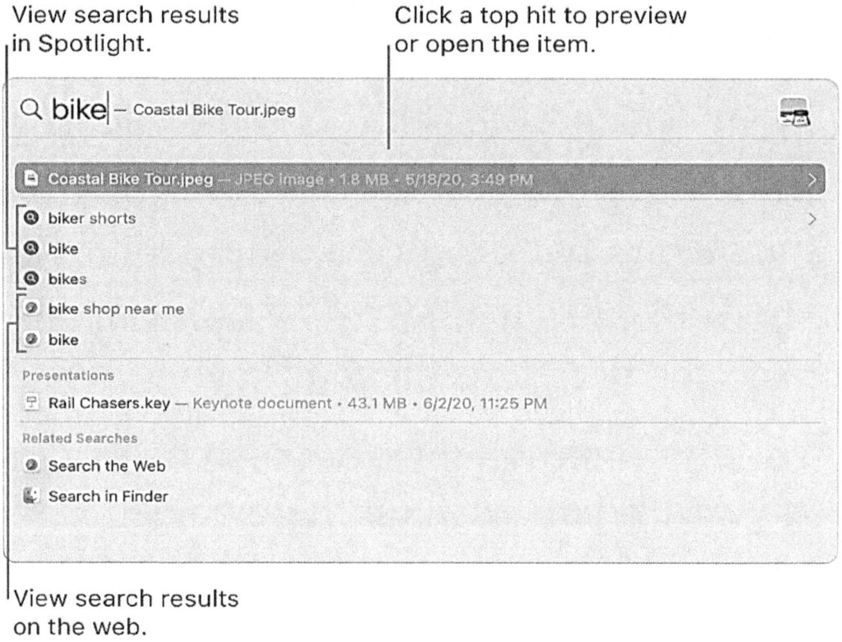

3. You can carry out any of these actions from the result displayed;

- *Show a preview:* Click on the Tab key. Click on an app to view a list of files that you have opened recently, and then tap on a file to open such a file.
- *View results of a search suggested in Spotlight:* Tap on an item that follows

the Spotlight icon .

- *View results of a search suggested on the web:* Tap on an item that follows the Safari icon .
- *Open an item:* Click on the item twice.
- *Show a file location on your Mac:* Choose the file while you press and hold on the Command key. You will see the location of the file at the lower end of the preview.

The Control Center on Mac

Use Control Centre on Mac

The Control Centre on Mac computers provide easy access to important macOS system settings — like the volume, Wi-Fi, brightness, or Do Not Disturb. The control center can be customized in order to be able to access some other items, like the Fast User switching or the accessibility shortcuts.

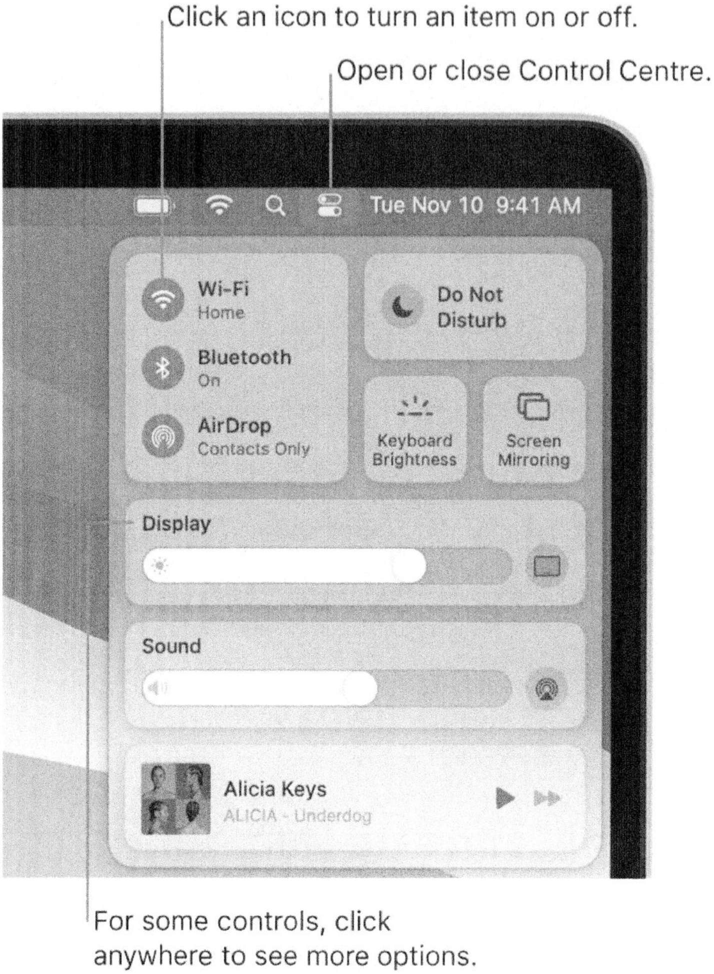

Using the Control Center

1. From your Mac, tap on Control Center from the menu bar.
2. The Control Center has a slider for different features. You can drag the slider to adjust settings for the feature. For

instance, you can adjust volume by dragging the volume slider, and you can also adjust brightness with the brightness slider. To access more options, tap on anywhere in the item or tap on the arrow > from the right.

Tip: Items, apps or features that you mostly used can be dragged to the menu bar from the Control Center to allow easy accessibility to those apps and features. To remove or delete the item from your menu bar, you can simply press and hold on the Command key while the item is being dragged out of your menu bar.

Customizing the Control Centre

1. On the Mac, click on the Apple menu, select "System Preferences," and then tap on "Dock & Menu Bar."
2. Click on a section from the sidebar to view items that you can add or to see items that are always in the Control Center.

- *Control Centre:* The features or items from this place are always displayed in Control Centre; and you won't be able to even remove them. Click on an item from the sidebar to see the item's preview in the Control Center found on the right.
- *Other Modules:* The items in this place can be added to the Control Center. Choose an item from the sidebar and then toggle on the "Show in Control Center" box for the item.

To add an item from the menu bar for quick access, click on the item's "Show in Menu Bar" checkbox.

Items in the **Menu bar only** cannot be added to the Control Center.

Using Siri on your machine

Use Siri on Mac for most of your everyday assignments, like obtaining fast answers to questions, playing music or video on your device and lots more. Siri can attend to almost anything when asked, for instance; "Hey Siri, set up the alarm for 9 AM" or ask "Hey Siri, can you tell me the meaning of game?

Siri can even give you suggestions from some apps even when you don't even request such. For instance, when the Safari browser send you invitation in Mail app, the Siri can suggest you add such invite to the Calendar for proper action when due.

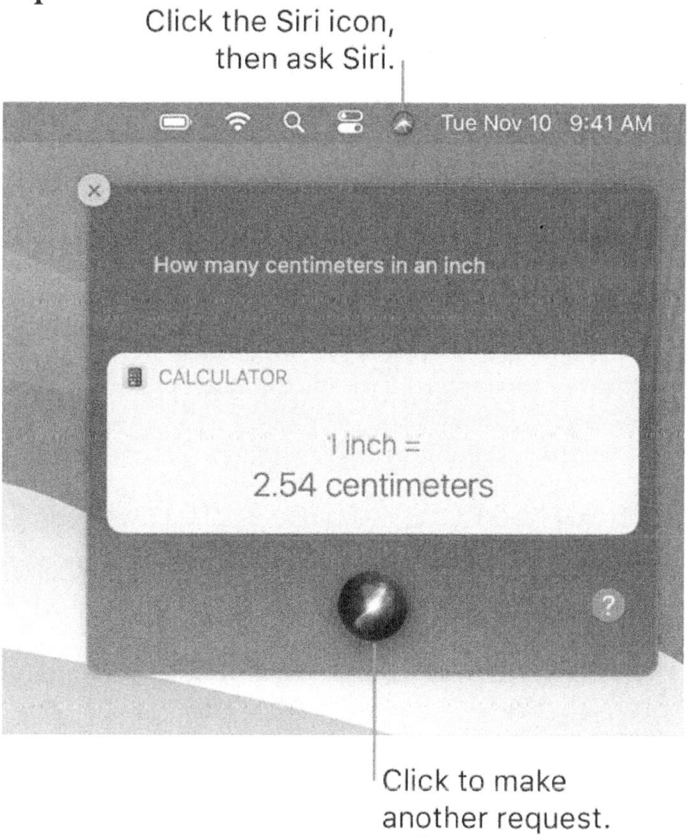

Turn on Siri

Siri can be turned on (if you want) during the initial setup of your Mac. But if you are unable to set up Siri then, you can still set it up now by following the basic steps below;

1. On the Mac, select Apple menu , click on "System Preferences,' and then tap on Siri.
2. Click on "Enable Ask Siri," if it has not been selected already, and then tap Enable.
3. When you are asked whether you will like to improve Siri and Dictation, you can do any of these;
    - *Share audio recordings:* Tap on Share Audio Recordings to enable Apple to save the audio recording of your interaction with Siri and Dictation. Samples of saved audio recordings can be reviewed by Apple for many reasons.
    - *Don't share audio recordings:* Select "Not Now."

When you change your mind in the future to start sharing or stop sharing Siri audio recording, simply go to the "Security & Privacy" > "Privacy preferences" > "Analytics & Improvements" and then select or unselect the "Improve Siri & Dictation" box.

Note: Any audio interaction you had with Siri can be deleted provided it is not more than six months old. To delete associated history for Siri and dictation;

- On your machine, click on Apple menu , select "System Preferences," and then tap Siri.
- Select "Delete Siri & Dictation History."
- Click on "Delete."

Carry out any of these actions;

- *Use "Hey Siri":* If the AirPods you are pairing with Mac or your Mac support voice, you can chose the Listen for "Hey Siri" tick box. And voice out "Hey Siri" to start using Siri. If you want to be able to use Siri even when your machine is locked or in sleeping mode, you can simply choose the "Allow Siri when locked" box.

- *Set a keyboard shortcut:* Click on the pop-up menu of the Keyboard Shortcut, and then select a shortcut to request Siri or you can even create your desired shortcut.

  Tip: If you can see the microphone icon in the function key on your keyboard, simply press and hold the icon to use Siri.

- *Indicate how you want Siri to communicate:* Tap on the Language pop-up menu, and then select a language. Click on Siri Voice pop-up option to select the gender (and oftentimes the dialect) you want Siri to speak.

- *Mute Siri:* Tap "Off" beside the Voice Feedback — you will be able to see answers from Siri in the Siri window but no sound will be made.

- *Include Siri in the menu bar:* Click on the "Show Siri in menu bar" box.

Ask Siri

1. To request Siri on your computer, carry out any of these actions;

    - Press and then hold the microphone icon if you can see it in the function key on your keyboard.

      Note: Press and then hold if you wish to ask Siri any question; but you will need to press and release the to initiate Dictation.

    - Click on Siri from your menu bar. If you cannot see Siri in the menu, you can simply add it using the "Dock & Menu Bar preferences."

    - Click on Siri from the Touch Bar (for Mac that has a Touch Bar).

    - Voice out "Hey Siri" (this must be enabled in the Siri preferences; although this feature will only work if your Mac or headphone support it).

Request Siri to carry out a task for you.

Turning off Siri

1. From the Mac computer, click on Apple menu, select "System Preferences," and then tap "Siri."
2. Tap the "Enable Ask Siri" box to unselect it (disable).

Some basic Siri commands

Let us examine some basic Siri commands

1. Siri calls and texts

You can use Siri to send calls and send some important messages.

- Using Siri to call: just say "Hey Siri, call John on speaker" Siri will call John for you and put it on speaker.

- Use Siri to remind yourself to make some important calls: Siri looks for important calls that you have scheduled in your calendar and will notify you prior time.
- Use Siri to text: just say "Hey Siri, text Mercy that I am coming by 8 PM" or you say "Hey Siri, message Dad I will be home in 20 minutes on WhatsApp," or you say, "Hey Siri, read the last message from John."
- You can also use Siri for Facetime: say, "Hey Siri, Facetime Ricardo by 2PM".

2. Siri alarm, reminder, and timers

- Say, "Hey Siri, wake me up by 7 PM."
- Request Siri to remind you about a meeting. Say, "Hey Siri, remind me I have a meeting with the chancellor by 6PM."
- Siri setting timer for you. Just say, "Hey Siri, set a timer for 7 hour."

3. **Siri music:** Siri finds your best songs for you, and can even explore your favorite collections of music.
   - Say, "Hey Siri, play me a song from my favorites."
   - Asking Siri what year, a song was composed. Say, "Hey Siri, when did this song come out."
   - Asking Siri what song is this. Just say "Hey Siri, what song is playing currently"

Asking Siri to play you an artist's latest song. Just say "Hey Siri, play me John's latest song."

Use Notification Centre on Mac

In the Notification Centre on your machine, details of how your day is going can be accessed – like weather, birthday, appointments and probably a summary of what you planned to do the following day – and also catch up on missed notifications.

Open or close Notification Centre on your Mac

On your machine, you can carry out any of these actions;

- *Open Notification Centre:* Tap on the date and time from the menu bar, or swipe to the left with your two fingers from the right corner of the trackpad.
- *Close Notification Centre:* Tap anywhere on your desktop, tap the date and time from

the menu bar, or use your two fingers to swipe to the right.

Use notifications in Notification Centre on your Mac

In the Notification Centre, simply move your pointer over a particular notification, and then carry out one of the following:

- *Expand or collapse a stack of notifications:* Multiple notifications from apps with grouped notifications will be stacked. And to expand such stack and access all of the notifications, tap anywhere from the top notification. Click on "Show less" to collapse the stack.
- *Take action:* Tap on the action. For instance, select Snooze when you receive a notification from the Calendar app, or tap Reply when you receive a notification from your Mail app.

If there is an arrow next to a particular action, tap that arrow to access more options. For instance, to attend to a call from your Messages app, tap the arrow beside the "Decline," option and then select "Reply with Message."

- *See more details:* Tap on the specific notification to access the item from the app. If there is an arrow to the right side of the name of the app, tap that arrow to access details in that particular notification.
- *Change notification settings for an app:* If there is an arrow to the right side of the name of the app, tap on the arrow, select the More button, and then select an option:
  - *Deliver Quietly:* Tapping this means that you don't want your notification at the upper right side of your screen or on your lock screen, but you would rather want your notification in the Notification Center without any sound.
  - *Deliver Prominently:* Tapping this means that you want your notification at the upper right side of your screen or on

your lock screen, and in the Notification Center, and this time around with a sound.

- *Turn Off:* Tapping on this means that you don't want to be receiving notifications at all. But if you have a change of mind, and you want to turn the notifications on for your apps, simply click on Apple menu , select System Preferences, tap Notifications, choose the app on your left, and then select "Allow Notifications" on your right (blue shows that notifications have been turned on).
- *Notification Preferences:* Display the notification settings for the app in the Notification preferences.

Clear all notifications or a single notification in a stack: Tap on the Clear All button or the Clear button.

Use widgets in Notification Centre on your Mac

In your Mac's Notification Centre, you can carry out any of the actions below;

- *See more details:* Tap anywhere you want in a widget if you want to access the related web page, app or preferences. For instance, tap anywhere you want in the Clock widget to access the Date & Time preferences, or tap anywhere you want from the Reminders widget to access the Reminders app.
- *Remove a widget:* Quickly press and then hold the Mac's Option key while you continue to move your pointer over that particular widget that you want to remove, and then tap on the Remove button .

How to customize Notification Center on Mac

1. On your machine, launch the Notification Center, and then tap Edit Widgets at the lower end of the screen.
2. Carry out any of the actions below;
   - *Locate a widget:* Utilize the search bar to look for any widget, or tap a category, like Clock, if you wish to preview the available widgets.
   - *Add a widget:* From your widget preview, select a size (if it is available), and let your pointer hover over that particular widget in the preview, then

     tap on the "Add button." The widget will be added to the right where the active widgets are found.
   - *Rearrange widgets:* To rearrange a particular widget, simply drag that widget to a new location.

- *Edit a widget:* From your list of active widgets, hover your pointer over that particular widget that you want to edit (you will see "Edit Widget" appearing below the name of the widget), then tap anywhere in the widget. The widget will flip to show settings that you can customize — for instance, the list in the remainder widget can be changed. When you are satisfied with the editing, select "Done."
- *Resize a widget:* From your active widgets, Control-click any widget, and then select another size.
- *Remove an active widget:* Hover your pointer over any active widget, and then tap on the Remove button .

When you finished, click on "Done" at the lower end of your active widgets.

How to pause or stop notifications on Mac

Many in-built or third party apps on your machine deploy notifications to notify you about any update, event or changes. The Notifications will be directed to the right edge of your desktop, and might stay there until you close them.

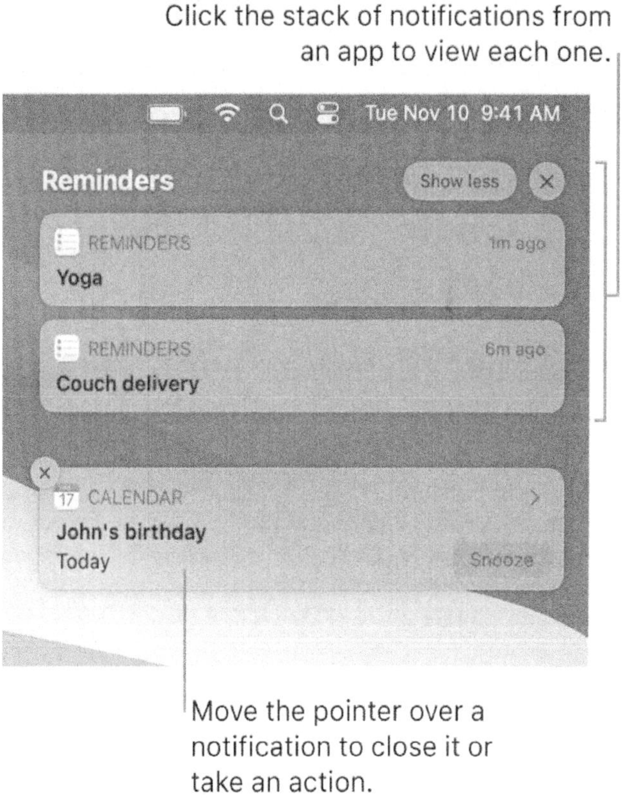

Pause notifications

1. On your machine, select Apple menu, tap on System Preferences, and then choose Notifications.

2. In the Notifications preferences, choose "Do Not Disturb" from the left menu, and then set the options.

   When you have turned on the "Do Not Disturb," you will see the "Do Not Disturb icon " in the menu bar. You won't be able to view or hear the sound of notifications as they come, because they are saved automatically in the Notification Center where they can be accessed later.

The "Do Not Disturb" feature can be turned on quickly by using the Control Center. To do this, you can simply press and then hold the Option key while clicking on the date and time from the menu bar, or simply press the crescent shaped symbol (if you can see it on your keyboard).

How to stop notifications on Mac

1. On your machine, select Apple menu , tap on System Preferences, and then choose Notifications.

2. In the Notifications preferences, choose an app from the left, and then unselect the "Allow Notifications" for that particular app.

   All the other notification options for that app will be dimmed. Notifications from the app will be stopped until you enable the "Allow Notifications" again for the app.

Set sleep and wake settings for your Mac

You can enable settings for your machine to go to sleep once a specific time of inactivity has been reached. You can as well indicate a specific time that you want Mac to go to sleep and wake.

Note: Some options and settings described below may be unavailable depending on the type of Mac you are using.

Specify sleep and wake settings for a Mac desktop computer

1. On your machine, select Apple menu , tap on System Preferences, and then tap Energy Saver.
2. Carry out any of these actions;
   - *Set time for Mac to go to sleep and wake up:* Tap on Change Settings (beside Proxies) to launch the Network pane of System Preferences.
   - *Set the quantity of time that your computer or display should wait before going to sleep:* Drag the slider for the "Computer sleep" and the "Display sleep."
   - *Prevent Mac from automatically going to sleep:* Choose "Prevent computer from sleeping automatically when the display is off"".

- *Let the hard disks go to sleep:* Click on "Put hard disks to sleep when possible."
- *Let your machine remain turned on anytime power is available:* Click on "Start up automatically after a power failure".
- *Let Mac update system while sleeping:* Click on Battery, and then choose "Enable Power Nap."
- *Let Mac wake briefly so that users will be able to access shared services (if applicable):* Select Power Adapter, and then choose any of the "Wake for..." options that are available, like the "Wake for network access".

Specify sleep and wake settings for a Mac notebook

- On your machine, click on Apple menu, tap System Preferences, and then choose Battery.

- Carry out any of these actions;
  - *Set time for Mac to go to sleep and wake up:* Tap on Schedule, and then choose the options you need. To schedule a time for your Mac to wake up and sleep, follow the steps below;
    - On your machine, click on Apple menu , tap System Preferences, choose Battery, and then tap on Schedule.
    - Choose the options that you wish to use.
      - *Set a wake time or a startup time for your Mac:* Choose the "Start up or wake" box. Select a day or group of days, input a time, and then select Apply.
      - *Set a shutdown, sleep, or restart time for your Mac:* Click on the "Sleep, restart or shut down" box and select the right option from the displayed menu. Select a day or group of days, input a desired time, and then select Apply.

- *Move between graphics modes:* Tap on Power Adapter or Battery, and then choose "Automatic graphics switching" to automatically move between graphics modes to have a better battery life.
- *Set sleep times for the time you are using the battery of your Mac Notebook:* Select Battery, and then drag the slider for "Turn display off after."
- *Set sleep times for the time you are using the Power Adapter of your Mac Notebook:* Select Power Adapter, and then drag the slider for "Turn display off after."
- *Prevent Mac from automatically going to sleep:* Click on Power Adapter, and then choose "Prevent computer from sleeping automatically when the display is off".
- *Let the hard disks go to sleep:* Select Power Adapter or Battery, and then click on "Put hard disks to sleep when possible".

- *Let the display be dimmed when you are using Mac's battery:* Select Battery, and then choose "Slightly dim the display while on battery power".
- *Let Mac update system while sleeping:* Click on Battery, and then choose "Enable Power Nap while on battery power". Select Power Adapter, and then choose "Enable Power Nap while plugged into a power adapter".
- *Let Mac wake briefly so that users will be able to access shared services (if applicable):* Select Power Adapter, and then choose any of the "Wake for..." options that are available, like the "Wake for network access."

How to put your machine to sleep or wake it up

There are times when your Mac will be idle (you are not using the computer), saving energy for later use can be achieved by putting your machine to sleep. When you put your machine to sleep, it is still turned on but won't be using much power. The Mac takes less amount of time to wake up from sleep than it takes to come up after being powered off.

Put your Mac to sleep

Carry out any of these actions if you want your Mac to sleep;

- Click on Apple menu, and select "Sleep."
- If you are using a Mac Notebook, close your display.
- If you have a Mac that has a CD and DVD drive, click the Option-Command-Media Eject key ⏏.

  Tip: In case the Mac you are using has Touch Bar, the sleep button can be added to the Control Strip. To do this, click on the Apple menu, select System Preferences, choose Keyboard, tap on the Keyboard button, and then choose Customize

Control Strip. Then Drag the Sleep button onto the Touch Bar.

Wake your Mac from sleep

Carry out any of the actions below to wake your machine from sleep;

- Press any key on your keyboard, or click the trackpad or the mouse.
- If you are using a Mac notebook, you can quickly wake your Machine from sleeping mode by opening the display.

Log out, restart or shut down your Mac

Whenever you want, you can log out of Mac, restart Mac or even shut Mac down.

Log out

- On your computer, click on Apple menu and select Log Out.

  When you log out of your machine, all of the apps windows that are opened before logging out will be opened and you can always continue from where you stopped. However, if you do not want these app windows to reopen when your machine logs out, simply unselect the "Reopen windows when logging back in".

Restart

- On your machine, click on Apple menu and choose Restart.

  When your machine restarts, all of the apps windows that are opened before restarting will be opened and you can always continue from where you stopped. However, if you don't want these app windows to reopen when your machine restarts, simply unselect the "Reopen windows when logging back in".

Shut down

- On your machine, click on Apple menu and choose Shut Down.

Your machine is only fully shut down once you see that the screen has turned black.

Some machines won't display a power light, and some don't have fan nor drive noise.

Caution: If what you are using is a Mac notebook, you are advised to wait for the machine to properly shut down (goes black) before you close the display. If you don't wait for the machine to shut down fully before you close the display (closing the display while your machine is still in the process of shutting down), your machine might not shut down effectively and might affect its working condition when next you power on Mac.

In addition, you should always endeavor to shut down the Mac before you open the case when you want to install other devices or some extra memory in the computer. Also, you should try and shut down your Mac when you want to attach or disconnect some peripheral devices.

You don't have to shut the Mac down when you are connecting or removing cables, like USB-C, Ethernet or Thunderbolt.

Note: You might want to force shutdown if it is necessary — for instance, when your machine becomes unnece-ssarily unrespo-nsive — by simply pressing and holding on the power button until the Mac shuts itself down. Some unsaved changes might be lost in the process, especially in opened documents.

What to do if an app freezes or quits itself unexpectedly on Mac

The following suggestions might be applicable when Mac stops working;

- If your app becomes frozen and unresponsive, click on Apple menu, select Force Quit, and click on that particular app from the displayed dialogue, then tap Force Quit. Some changes in the apps that are not saved before force quitting might be lost, and it might be difficult to get them back.

- If your app quits, you can reopen the app by tapping Reopen from the displayed dialogue.
- Click on the Apple menu, and then select "Restart" to restart Mac.
- The app might be one that is not compatible with the macOS 11, so you can simply check the details of the app from where you downloaded to confirm if it is actually compatible or not.
- Launch another file from the app. The original file might be the one with a problem.
- Check if there is an update to your software or the app.
- Remove any external devices that you must have connected to Mac (for instance, a printer). It is possible that macOS 11 does not support that particular external device.
- Uninstall some app plugins from third party makers.

Mac just won't go to sleep or stay in sleep?

If your machine can't just go to sleeping mode or it is just waking up unnecessarily even when you are not there, you might have to change some settings for the Sleep preferences. If the problem persists, then it is possible that something else is waking your gadget up unnecessarily.

- *Check your Mac's sleep settings:* You need to confirm that the sleeping mode settings are just the way they should be. To access the settings for the sleeping mode, click on Apple menu , select System Preferences, and then carry out any of these settings;
  - *If you have a Mac desktop computer:* Tap on Energy Saver. If you wish to indicate the quantity of time that must pass before Mac goes to sleeping mode, simply drag the slider for the "Computer sleep" and the "Display sleep."
  - *If you have a Mac notebook:* Select Battery, and then choose Power Ada-

pter or Battery. If you wish to indicate the quantity of time that must pass before Mac goes to sleeping mode, simply drag the slider for the "Turn display off after" setting. You can as well unselect the "Prevent computer from sleeping automatically when the display is off" from pane of the Power Adapter.

Check your Mac's network access setting: It is possible that some other users are the ones remotely waking up your Mac so that they can use your Mac's shared resources. If you want to disable things like this, click on Apple menu , select System Preferences, and then carry out any of these actions;

- *If you have a Mac desktop computer:* Tap on Energy Saver, and then unselect the "Wake for network access" option.
- *If you have a Mac notebook:* Select Battery, tap on Power Adapter, and then unselect the "Wake for network access" option.

Check your Mac's Bluetooth settings: Your Mac might be waking up unintentionally by Bluetooth devices. If you want to disable Bluetooth mouse or keyboard from waking up your Mac, simply click on Apple menu , select System Preferences, and then tap on Bluetooth. Choose Advanced, and then unselect the "Allow Bluetooth devices to wake this computer" option.

Check your Mac's sharing preferences: When there are people deploying shared services on Mac, your Mac might be unable to go to sleep. For instance, they might be using shared files stored on your Mac or using printers that have been previously connected to your Mac. To confirm that you have actually enabled the correct sharing preferences, click on Apple Menu

, select System Preferences, and then tap Sharing. And you can then disable any of the services that you are not using by unselecting the "On" box beside that particular service.

Check Mac's activity: Your Mac might be unable to go to sleep because of some heavy processes that are running in the Mac's background. You can confirm whether there is a process using the central processing unit of your computer by checking the Mac's activity monitor. To do this, simply launch the Finder window, scroll to Applications, select Utilities, tap on Activity Monitor and click on the CPU button located at the top of the screen.

Confirm if there is no other setting waking up your Mac: You can check any of these;

- *Unintended keyboard presses or mouse and trackpad clicks:* Unexpected key presses and unintended mouse or trackpad clicks can wake your Mac. Sometimes, Mac might wake up even when you don't wake it up (when you are not there); it is possible that something is pressing the Mac's track-pad, mouse or the keyboard keys.

- *Apps:* Some apps can access a disk, and these apps might be the one preventing your machine from going to sleep. For instance, a DVD player can access the optical disc drive of Mac when it wants to play films, and Music can access disk to access the songs it is playing.
- *Spotlight indexing:* Mac will be unable to go to sleeping mode when Spotlight is indexing hard disk. To see if Spotlight is indexing the hard disk, simply open the Spotlight. In addition, depending on the quantity of files on your Mac, the indexing process can take longer than necessary.
- *Connected storage and devices:* Your Mac might be unable to go to sleep due to Thunderbolt and USB malfunctioning. To see if these attached devices are the problem, simply remove them and see if Mac will be able to go to sleep. If your Mac does go to sleep, re-attach each of the items one after the other so

that you will be able to figure out which of them is actually malfunctioning.

Share your Mac resources when it's in sleep

You can decide to set your gadget to wake up from sleeping mode when there are other users accessing your Mac's shared resources, especially when resources like Shared printers are involved.

To enjoy this feature, an Apple wireless device-supporting 802.11n and with the latest installed firmware is required.

Share resources for a Mac desktop computer

1. On your gadget, click on Apple menu, select System Preferences, and then click on Energy Saver.
2. Choose from any of the "Wake for..." options that are available like the "Wake for Ethernet network access."

Share resources for a Mac notebook

If you have the Mac notebook, you will need to plug it inside a Power adapter.

1. On your gadget, click on Apple menu, select System Preferences, and then click on Battery > Power Adapter.
2. Choose from any of the "Wake for..." options that are available like the "Wake for network access".

When you have ticked the "Wake for network access" box, the Mac will be waking up at these times;

- When your Mac's shared items are being accessed by another using another computer.
- At consistent intervals to allow your machine to tell other computers when its resources are available on the network.

CHAPTER THREE

MacOS Big Sur Desktop

The Menu bar is found at the top side of your screen, while at the lower end of the screen is where you can find the Dock. The **desktop** is the space in between the menu bar and the Dock, and that is where you will be doing most of your works.

Use multiple desktops

Organize your tasks on desktop by creating extra spaces on the desktop. For instance, you can be sending mail to a colleague on a desktop, while writing with the note app on another desktop, and you can conveniently switch between the two desktops. Each desktop can even be customized individually to correlate with the task you are currently working on.

Work in multiple spaces on Mac

If the desktop on your machine becomes cluttered with too many app windows opened, Mission Control can be used to have extra desktops, named **spaces,** and top properly organize the windows. While working in a space, you will only be able to see the windows that are located in that space.

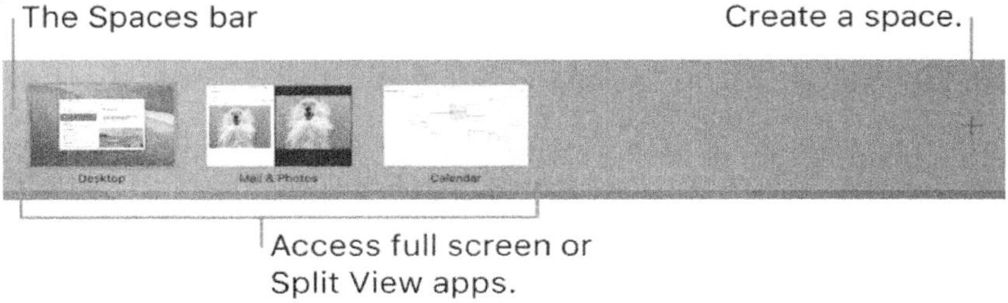

Create a space

1. On your machine, launch the Mission Control. To launch the Mission Control;

Enter or leave Mission Control

- *From your trackpad:* To enter the Mission Control, simply swipe up on the screen with three fingers. To leave the Mission Control, quickly swipe down on the screen.
- *From a keyboard:* To bring or dismiss the Mission Control, click on the Mission Control key or you can simply press the Control-Up Arrow.

  If you're working with apps in full screen or Split View, their thumbnails are shown in the Spaces bar.

2. Tap on the "Add button " from the Spaces bar.
3. When you are done, click on the thumbnail for any space to access that space.

Move between spaces

On your computer, you can carry out any of these actions:

- On your trackpad, quickly swipe to the left or to the right with three or four of your fingers. If it is a Magic Mouse, simply swipe with any of your two fingers.
- Click the Control key together with the Right or Left arrow key.

How to move an app window from one space to another

On your computer, carry out any of the actions below;

- You can simply drag the window of the app that you want to move to the corner of your screen, and the window will move automatically to the next space after a brief moment.
- Scroll to the space having the window that you plan to move, bring the Mission Control, and then drag that window up to that space that you plan to use.

You will be able to use the app in Split View if you are able to drag the window over a full screen app in the Spaces bar.

Delete a space

1. On your computer, bring the "Mission Control," and then hover your pointer to the top corner of your screen.
2. Hover your pointer over the particular space that you plan to delete in the Spaces bar and then select the "Delete button" that will show.

If you no longer wish to continue using a particular app in Split View or full screen, you can simply hover your pointer on the app thumbnail in the Space bar, and then select the "Exit button " that will come up.

Let your iPad be the second display for your Mac

With Sidecar, your iPad in the landscape position can be used as the second display (screen) for your Mac. What this means is that you will be able to extend the Mac's desktop capability by displaying various windows or apps on the iPad, or rather make your iPad display the same desktop you have on Mac.

Note: Just like most other Continuity features, the Sidecar feature requires the use of your Bluetooth and Wi-Fi. This means that Bluetooth and Wi-Fi must be enabled on your machine, and your Mac must meet system specifications.

How to set Sidecar option

One thing you should ensure first is that you use the same Apple ID to sign in on your iPad and on your Mac.

1. On your machine, click on Apple menu, select System Preferences, and then click on Sidecar.

2. Set the options for displaying the sidebar (by tapping on the tickbox to reveal the sidebar on the iPad, and then select a location from the pop-up menu.) and the Touch Bar (by tapping on the tickbox to reveal the Touch bar on the iPad, and then select a location from the pop-up menu.) on iPad, and also for using Apple Pencil.

3. If you have not been connected to your iPad already, simply tap on the "Connect to" pop-up menu, and then select your iPad.

   You can as well connect to your iPad by using the Display in the Control Center , or by deploying the Display menu from the menu bar (if you can see the menu), or by deploying the AirPlay Display pop-up menu from the Displays preferences.

To utilize the Sidecar feature, you don't need a cable to connect iPad with Mac.

Use Sidecar

1. If you have not been connected to your iPad already, simply tap on Display from the Control Centre or by deploying the Display menu from the menu bar (if you can see the menu).

   You will see the Sidecar menu appe-aring in your menu bar. Whenever you want, it is very easy to change the way you work with your iPad from your Sidecar menu. For instance, you can switch between using your iPad as a separate display or as a mirrored, or display or conceal your sidebar or Touch Bar on your iPad

2. Carry out any of the actions below;

   - *Move windows from your Mac to the iPad:* Make the pointer to show up on your iPad by dragging a window straight to the edge of your screen.

Alternatively, while working with an app, you can simply select Window, and click on "Move Window to iPad."

- *Move windows from iPad to Mac:* Make the pointer to show up on your Mac by dragging a window straight to the edge of your screen. Alternatively, while working with an app, you can simply select Window, and click on "Move Window back to Mac."
- *Use the sidebar on your iPad:* Using any of your finger or Apple Pencil, click on icons from the sidebar to; reveal or conceal the menu bar, display or conceal the Dock, or reveal your onscreen keyboard. Or click on one or more modifier keys, like the Ctrl , to enjoy the keyboard shortcuts.
- *Utilize the Touch Bar on your iPad:* With any of your finger or Apple Pencil, click on any button from your Touch Bar. The buttons you see will vary depending on the task or app.

- *Use Apple Pencil on your iPad:* Using the Apple Pencil, tap on an item to select the item like files, tick boxes or menu commands. If the Apple Pencil supports drawing tools (and you have already set the option in the Sidecar preferences), you can tap twice on the bottom of your Apple Pencil to deploy drawing tools in some of your apps.

- *Use gestures on iPad:* Deploy some basic gestures, like swipe, zoom, scroll and tap, including some basic gestures for editing and entering your texts.

- *Switch between Mac desktop and the iPad on iPad:* Simply swipe up from the lower edge of the iPad using one finger to reveal your Home Screen. To display your iPad Dock, quickly swipe up and then pause. You can also bring the App Switcher by swiping up and then pause in the middle of your screen. To go back to your Mac desktop, quickly swipe up, and then tap on the Sidecar icon .

When you want to stop using the iPad, click on the Disconnect icon located at the lower end of the sidebar on your iPad.

You can equally disconnect on Mac by tapping on the active iPad in the Sidecar menu from your menu bar.

Use the Dock on Mac

Launch your apps from the Dock, and have easy access to your most used apps from the Dock.

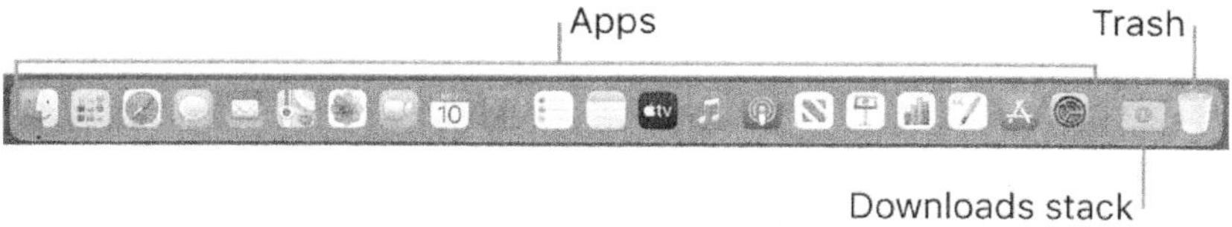

The Dock is able to display up to three of your recently used apps, and will create a separate folder for downloaded items from the web. Your Dock is found along the lower end of your screen, but you will be able to set it to show along the right or left edge of your screen.

Open items in the Dock

Carry out any of these actions from the Dock;

- *Open an app:* Tap on the icon of the app that you wish to open. For instance, tap on the Finder icon  to open Finder in your Dock.
- *Open a file in an app:* Drag such file over the icon of an app. For instance, you can access a document created in Pages by dragging such a document over the Pages icon in your Dock.
- *Show an item in the Finder:* Command-click on the icon of that item.
- *Switch to the previous app and hide the current app:* Option-click on the icon of the current app.
- *Switch to another app and hide all other apps:* Option-Command-click on app icon that you wish to switch to.

Take other actions for items in the Dock

You can carry out any of these actions in the Dock;

- *Show a shortcut menu of actions:* Control-click on an item to show its shortcut menu, and then select an action from the list, like **Show Recents**, or tap a filename to access the file.
- *Force an app to quit:* If you notice that one of your apps has stop responding effectively, simply Control-click on the app icon and then tap "Force Quit." This may cause you to lose some changes that you have not properly saved on your Mac.

Add, remove or rearrange Dock items

On your Mac, do any of the following:

- *Add any app or item to your Dock:* Drag any app that you want to put in Dock to the left edge of that tiny line (see below) that divide the recently used apps. The item's alias will be put in the Dock.

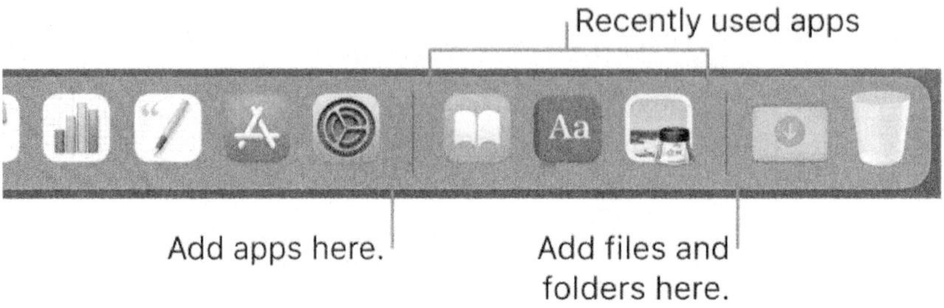

- *Remove an item from the Dock:* Drag the item out of the Dock until you see Remove. Only the alias is removed; the actual item remains on your Mac.

  In the case of accidental removal of an app icon in the Dock, you can easily put the app icon since the app will still be on your Mac. To place the icon back in the Dock, simply Control-click on the app icon, select **options** and tap "**Keep in Dock.**"

- *Rearrange items in the Dock:* An item in the Dock can be rearranged by dragging such item to another location.

Customize the Dock

1. On your computer, click on Apple menu, select System Preferences, and then tap on Dock & Menu Bar preferences.

2. From the Dock & Menu Bar section found in the sidebar, you will be able to change any option you want to change.

   For instance, the appearance of an item can be changed, hide the item, adjust the size of the item and even locate the item along the right corner or left edge of your screen.

   To get more details about the options, tap on the Help button  located in the pane.

Tip: You can adjust the size of the Dock by hovering your pointer over the line separator in the dock until you see a double arrow, then click the pointer and drag it up or down. You will be able to access some other shortcut menus when you Control-click the line of separator.

You can even use the keyboard shortcut to move to your Dock. On your keyboard, press Control-F3 (Control-Fn-F3 if you have a Mac notebook) to navigate to your Dock. Then move from one icon to another by using the

Right arrow key and the left arrow key. Tap the "**Return**" key to launch an item.

When you see a red badge on any of your app icons in the Dock, it is literally telling you that you need to take a specific action concerning the app. For instance, when you see the red badge on your Mail icon in the Dock, it means that you have a new email message. Simply click on the app icon to launch the app and attend to the issue.

Dock in Mac contains a question mark: what does it mean?

If there is an app you deleted from your Mac, and such app has its icon in the Dock, the icon will remain in your Dock only that it will be covered with a question mark. If you want to remove the question mark, simply drag that particular app icon out of your Dock until there is a "Remove" option, which you can tap to completely remove the question mark from Dock.

CHAPTER THREE

UNDERSTANDING THE MAC BASICS

Connect your Mac to the Internet

It is now very easy, more than before, to connect your Mac to the internet while at home, on the move or at work. The two most common methods of enjoying the internet on Mac are by connecting with a Wi-Fi or using an Ethernet connection (this is a wired connection). If none of these two options is available, you can use an Instant Hotspot.

Use Wi-Fi

Once your Mac sees an available Wi-Fi connection, it will display the Wi-Fi icon  in its menu bar located at the top area of your screen. Tap the Wi-Fi icon, and then pick a network you want to join. If there is a lock icon  beside the name of the network, it means that the network is being protected with a password. Do not guess this password.

Try to ask the owner of the Wi-Fi to give you the password. To enjoy internet on Mac with Wi-Fi, follow the steps below;

Join a public Wi-Fi network

1. On your machine, click on your Wi-Fi icon  from the menu bar, and then select the network that you wish to join.

   If you cannot see your desired network, tap "Other Networks" to bring networks that are nearby.

2. If asked, input the password for that network, and then click on "Join."

Join a hidden Wi-Fi network

You have to know the name of the hidden network, the network's security protocol and the network's password before you will be able to safely join the network.

1. On your machine, click on your Wi-Fi icon from the menu bar, tap "Other Networks," and then click on "Other" at the lower end of the list of "Other Networks."
2. Input network's name inside the Name field of the Network.
3. Click on the Security pop-up menu, and then select the type of the wireless security, which the network is using.
4. Input the details for any extra fields that might be prompted, like the username and password, and then click on "Join."

Use Ethernet

An Ethernet network, a cable modem, or a DSL can be used to connect Mac to the internet. If there is an Ethernet connection available, simply use the Ethernet port on Mac to connect Mac to an Ethernet cable. The Ethernet connection is usually identified by the symbol . In an instance that Mac does not have an Ethernet port, simply buy an adapter to safely connect the cable to your Mac's USB or Thunderbolt port. To connect Mac to the internet using an Ethernet option, follow the steps below;

1. Safely connect your Mac's Ethernet port to a network device (like a router or a switch) or a modem by using an Ethernet cable. If your Mac does not have an in-built Ethernet port, buy a USB to Ethernet adapter, or use a Thunderbolt to Gigabit Ethernet adapter.

   In some instances, connection is made automatically to the internet. Otherwise, follow the steps below to input settings for your network. If you don't know the settings to enter, contact your internet service provider or network administrator.

2. On your machine, click on Apple menu , select System Preferences, and then click on "Network."

3. On the available list from the left, choose Ethernet.
4. Click on the pop-up menu of the Configure IPv4, and then select the approved configuration method of your ISP.
   - *Using DHCP:* Select this option if you have automatically gotten an IP address from your internet service provider.
   - *Using DHCP with manual address:* Select this option if you have gotten a specific IP address, and your internet service provider also uses DHCP or some other network settings.
   - *Using BootP:* Select this option if your ISP deploys BootP.
   - *Manually:* Select this option if you have gotten a specific router address, a subnet mask and an IP address from your internet service provider.

Click on "Advanced," select "DNS," tap on the Add button + located just below DNS

Servers, and then input the address of Mac's ISP DNS server.

If your internet service provider avails you with some search domain addresses, kindly input them also. Although, you might not necessarily need this if you have already configured Mac's IP settings to utilize DHCP.

If your service provider is able to provide you with other settings like proxy server, IPv6, or extra Ethernet settings, simply tap "Advanced" to explore them.

Select OK to activate the settings for Ethernet service.

Use Instant Hotspot

Sometimes, you might not have direct access to an Ethernet connection or a Wi-Fi access, but you will be able to enjoy the internet using your Mac and Instant Hotspot, where you can connect using your iPad's or iPhone's personal Hotspot.

Your Mac is able to deploy the personal hotspot of your iPad or iPhone (Wi-Fi + Cellular model) to enjoy the internet provided your Mac and your iPad or iPhone are within reasonable range from each other. Before you establish connection between your Mac and your iPhone/iPad, ensure the personal hotspot of the iPhone or iPad is turned on by going to **Settings,** and then tap on **Personal Hotspot** on your iPhone or iPad. But you have to know that additional charges may be incurred on your iPad or iPhone depending on carriers. To connect your Mac with your iOS or iPadOS devices, follow the steps below;

Connect using Wi-Fi

1. Confirm that your iPhone or iPad device and Mac are securely signed in to iCloud using the same Apple ID.
2. From your Mac, tap on the Wi-Fi icon from your menu bar, and then select your iPad or iPhone.

Once a stable connection has been established between your Mac and your iPhone's or iPad personal hotspot, the Wi-Fi status menu can be deployed to check your Mac's battery level/status and the mobile strength signal. When you are no longer using the Hotspot, Mac will automatically disconnect itself from the connection in order to save battery life.

Wi-Fi not available in Network preferences on Mac?

If your Mac has Wi-Fi features but you are unable to access Wi-Fi in your Network preferences, it is likely that you have not set up the Wi-Fi service yet. To do this, follow the steps below;

1. On your machine, click on Apple menu, select System Preferences, and then click on "Network."

2. Click on the Add button + located at the lower end of the list.
3. Click on the Interface pop-up menu, and then select Wi-Fi.
4. Input the service's name, and then tap "Create."

   The service is usually named Wi-Fi by default, but you can change the name if you wish.
5. Enter the right settings for your Wi-Fi service, like the name of the network, and then tap "Advanced" to adjust other settings.
6. To decide which of the service should be used first if there are more than one active services, click on the

   Action pop-up menu, and then click "Set Service Order," then change the order by dragging the network services in your list.

Browsing the internet with Safari on Mac

Go to a web page

1. Launch the Safari app on Mac, and then enter the name of the page or the URL of the page inside the **Smart Search field.** As you enter the address, Safari will keep offering you suggestions.

2. Select a suggestion, or press the Return key to go straight to the web address you entered.

Preview a link in a web page

1. Hold your pointer over a link in the Safari app on Mac.
2. The URL of the website will appear in the Status bar at the lower end of the window.
   - If you are unable to view the status bar, select View, and tap "Show Status Bar."

- You can also **force click** the link to see the content if the trackpad you are using supports it.

Search for items using Safari on Mac

With Safari, you can search almost anything you are looking for. As you enter words inside the Smart Search field, Safari will keep bringing you useful suggestions. You can take one of the Safari's suggestions or continue typing if what Safari suggested doesn't look like what you are looking for.

Start a search

1. In your Safari app  on Mac, input a phrase or a word inside the Smart Search field. As you enter the word, Safari will bring you useful suggestions.
2. Select a suggestion, or press the Return key to search anything with your chosen search engine.
   When you tap on a suggestion, your browser will direct you to the web page or

avail you with the interactive preview with handy information.

Hint: If you have turned on Safari in iCloud preferences on your iPad, iPod Touch and iPhone, Safari will show you suggestions from your opened websites, browsing history and bookmarks across your various devices.

Search the current web page

1. From the Safari app on Mac, press the Command-F.
2. Enter a word or phrase inside the search field you see at the top right edge.

   To view the next thing on the page, tap on the Next button to the left side of the field.

Start a search based on the current web page

- Launch your Safari app on your machine and input a letter or some letters inside the Smart Search box.

As you enter your texts, you will get instant Siri suggestions based on what is in the current web page.

Repeat a search

- From the Safari app on Mac, use your keyboard or highlight all the text to delete them inside the Smart Search field.
- Click on the magnifying glass.
- You will get a list where you can select your recent search.

You can repeat the last search by clicking on "History," and then choose "Search Results SnapBack."

Quickly search a site you visited before

- From the Safari app on Mac, input site's name, and then follow it by the name of your search term.

  For instance, you can enter "wiki baseball" to search Wikipedia for "baseball."

Switch search engines

- From the Safari app on Mac, use your keyboard or highlight all the text to delete them inside the Smart Search field.
- Click on the magnifying glass.
- Select a search engine that you want from the list. You will also be able to switch between search engines from the search pane of your Safari preferences.

Ways to improve your search result in Safari

Narrow your search

To narrow your search in the Safari app on Mac, you can consider these useful suggestions:

- *Inculcate specificity:* For instance, searching for "Fan" will bring results for any type of fan; while searching for "ceiling fan" will give you result for fan that can be attached to the ceiling only.

- *Search for an exact phrase:* Deploy quotation marks to look for the whole phrase rather than each word in the phrase. If you want to find an article titled "How to green clean an office", endeavor to deploy quotation marks in the phrase.

Simplify your search

To simplify search in the Safari app on Mac, you can consider these useful suggestions;

- *Leave out common words:* Common words and small words are usually disregarded by search engines. For instance, you will get the same result with a search term like; "call the painter", "call a painter", and "call painter."
- *Ignore capitalization:* Your search engine will always treat capitalized words and un-capitalized words as the same thing. For instance, "North America", "North

america," and "north america" will be treated by search engines to mean the same thing.

- *Skip word endings:* Your search engines will normally drop word endings. For instance, "buy dog" and "buying dog" will often bring the same result in the search engine.

Adjust volume for Mac

Turn your Mac volume up or down

- Adjust the volume on Mac by clicking on the Volume control from the menu bar, and then drag the volume slider to quickly adjust the volume.

  If you cannot see the Volume control in your menu bar, click on Apple menu, tap System Preferences, and then select Sound. Toggle on the "Show volume in menu bar" box.

Change the sound output settings on Mac

Mac will be able to output sound either through the Mac's internal speakers, display speaker, or through headphones, speakers or some other gadgets inserted into Mac or wirelessly through AirPlay.

1. On your computer, click on the Apple menu , select System Preferences, tap Sound, and then click on "Output."
2. Choose the device that you plan to use from the list of sound output devices.

   You will see the list of all of the sound output devices that are available for your Mac, devices you inserted into your Mac's sound port ( ), AirPlay devices and USB speakers.

   For any device type that you inserted into your Mac's sound port, select Headphones.
3. Carry out any of the actions below to control output settings for sound;

- *Adjust the sound balance:* Simply drag the slider for the Sound balance.
- *Adjust the volume:* Simply drag the slider for the Output volume.
- *Stop sound output:* Click on the "Mute" box.
- *Display a volume control in your menu bar:* Click on the "Show volume in menu bar" box so that you will be able to turn up the volume or turn down the volume from anywhere.

If you want to assign a separate volume for the alert sounds, tap "Sound Effects."

You can set many other volume options for Mac using the Setup app for the Audio MIDI, and this actually depends on the Mac you are using.

If you are using an app with in-built volume control (for instance Music app or the iMovie app), their volume can never be greater than the Mac's output volume; meaning that these apps cannot override the volume settings you initially set for your Mac in the Sound preferences.

Change the sound input settings on Mac

Your Mac may come with one or more sound ports depending on the model of Mac that you are using. If your machine came with separate ports for the sound input and the sound output, the port for the input may either use a sound input icon or a microphone icon. For input sound, you will be able to use the Mac's internal microphone, the display microphone, or a microphone plugged inside the Mac's sound port.

1. On your machine, click on Apple menu , select "System Preferences," tap Sound, and then click on "Input."

   Note: The options you see here actually depend on the model of your Mac and the audio device you plugged to the Mac.

2. Choose the device that you wish to use from the list of your sound input devices.

All of the sound input devices that your Mac can use will be listed.

3. Carry out any of the settings below to set sound input settings;

   - *Adjust the input volume:* Drag the slider for the volume.

     If you are using your Mac's sound port to record sound, the input volume can be adjusted in order to duly compensate for the source of sound being too quiet or too loud.

     For instance, if you are recording some loud sounds, you can just reduce the input volume so that the recorded sound will not be too distorted or too loud. However, if you are capturing sound for someone who is talking softly, you can raise the input volume so that your Mac can capture the person's voice better.

   - *Capture little background noise when using your Mac's built-in microphone:* Choose "Use ambient noise reduction”. This setting will not be available if you have selected a 4-channel built-in microphone format in the Audio MIDI setup.

Note: You won’t be able to adjust input volume for any digital input device that is using your Mac’s controls. Input volume for devices like this can only be adjusted from its source (e.g a receiver).

Change the alert sounds on Mac

You will usually get an alert message on your screen anytime you attempt to do something that is not compatible with Mac, or when your computer needs your attention. An alert sound will always accompany the alert notification, which you can always change and adjust as you wish.

1. On Mac, click on Apple menu, select System Preferences, tap Sound, and then choose Sound Effects.

2. Click on an alert from the list to choose an alert sound. The alert you selected will play immediately so that you will be able to hear how it sounds.

   The alert plays when you select it so you can hear how it sounds.

3. Carry out any of the actions below in order to adjust sound for the alert;

   - *Change where you hear alerts:* If you want to use another output device to hear your alerts aside from the Mac's in-built speaker, simply select the output device from the "Play sound effects through" pop-up menu.

   - *Adjust the volume of alerts:* Drag the slider for the Alert volume. The alert volume is also a function of the output volume of your Mac, so the alert sound will automatically be lowered once you reduce the volume of your Mac.

   - *Initiate playing a sound when your computer starts up:* To listen to the startup sound anytime you restart Mac, choose the "Play sound on startup" box.

- *Decide whether you want to hear user interface sound effects:* Your computer usually play some sound effects anytime you carry out some actions, like dragging an app/file to the Trash. Unselect the "Play user interface sound effects" box if you want to disable this sound effect.
- *Decide whether you want to hear a sound effect when you change the volume:* On most keyboards, when you click on one of the keyboard's volume keys, the alert sound will play to enable you listen to the new volume. To disable this sound, un-select the "Play feedback when volume is changed" box. You will be able to reverse this setting temporarily by holding down the Shift key while pressing a volume key.

Change your Mac display's brightness

There is an option to adjust your Display's brightness manually or automatically. To do this, follow the steps below;

Use the brightness function keys

If your Mac's screen appears too dark or too bright, the Display's brightness can be adjusted to increase or decrease the brightness.

- On your machine, click on the brightness increase key ☼ or the brightness decrease key ☼.

How to adjust Brightness automatically

1. If your model of Mac has the **ambient light sensor**, select Apple menu , tap on System Preferences, choose Displays, and then click on "Display."
2. Choose "Automatically adjust brightness".

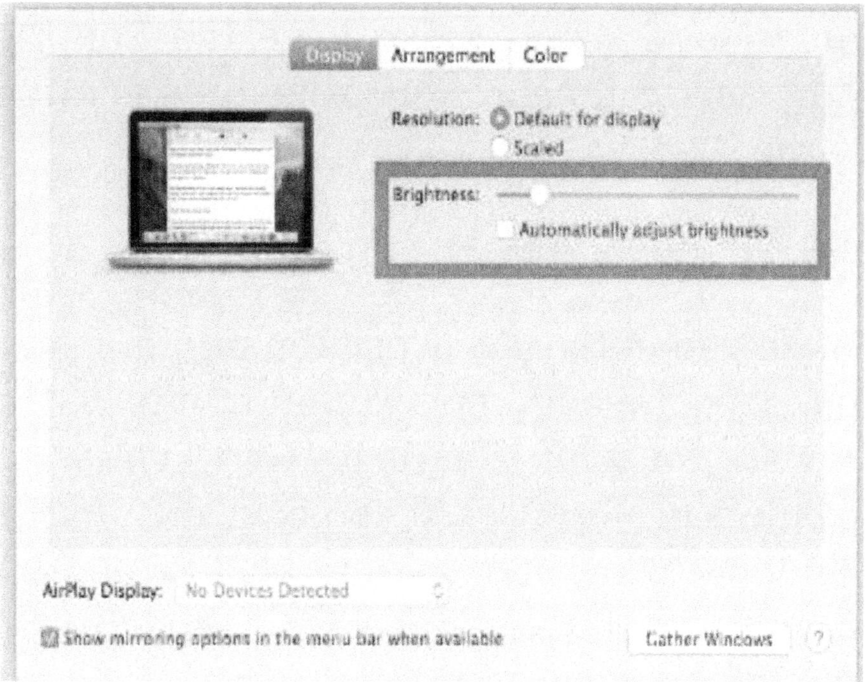

If your Mac does not have the "Automatically adjust brightness" box, then you should use the option to adjust the Brightness manually as described below.

How to adjust Brightness manually

1. On Mac, click on the Apple menu, select System Preferences, choose Displays, and then click on "Display."
2. Adjust the brightness for your display by using the Brightness slider.

Some Mac's display also have the Contrast Slider that can be used to adjust the contrast for the Display.

Add a printer on Mac

To conveniently use a printer on your Mac, you need to add the printer to the list of printers on your Mac using the Printers & Scanners preferences. If you have ever used a Windows computer before, the Printers & Scanners preferences is very similar to the Printing control panel in the Windows computers.

In some cases, macOS deploys AirPrint to connect to a printer or download the printer's software (printer driver) when you want to add your printer to Mac. Do not try to install the software that accompanied your printer or install the printer from the manufacturer's website. Use any of the instructions that suit you below and macOS will direct you to download the latest printer's software if it is required.

Printers that are AirPrint enabled are automatically compatible with Mac, but if your own printer is not AirPrint enabled, your Mac will automatically install the driver for it.

Add a USB printer

Adding USB printers is the simplest, as all that you need to do is to update the software and then attach the printer to Mac. macOS will detect the printer automatically and then download any required software to aid smooth printing. For most other printers, you might be required to add the printer by completing some steps below;

1. *On Mac, update your software:* Click on Apple menu, tap System Preferences, select Software Update, and then proceed to install any software that requires an update (list of software that needs to be updated will be provided). This step might be necessary even when Mac doesn't come up with any list to be updated, as it ensures that your Mac has the updated

information about any printer software available from Apple. If you don't update software, you might be prompted with a message that the software is not available when you want to connect your printer to Mac.

2. *Prepare your printer:* Unpack your printer according to the manufacturer's guide that came with the printer. You might need to install toner or ink, and also add paper. Then proceed to turn on your printer and ensure that it is not showing errors.
3. *Connect your printer:* Attach the USB cable of the printer to your Mac. If you get a prompt asking you to download new software, ensure that you download and install the software appropriately.

Add a Wi-Fi or network printer

There might be instances where your printer and your Mac are connected over the same Wi-Fi network. If this is the case, then your printer might be able to print without any formal setting. To confirm, select “File,” tap “Print,” click on the Printer pop-up menu, select “Nearby Printers” or “Printers & Scanners preferences,” and then select your printer. If your model of printer is not available, you will be able to add it.

1. *On Mac, update your software (in case you do not have an AirPrint printer):* Click on Apple menu, tap System Preferences, select Software Update, and then proceed to install any software that requires an update (list of software that needs to be updated will be provided). This step might be necessary even when Mac doesn't come up with any list to be updated, as it ensures that your Mac has the updated information about any printer software available from Apple. If you don’t update software, you might be prompted with a message that the software is not available when you want to connect your printer to Mac. If your printer is AirPrint enabled, you do not have to check for any software update.

2. *Prepare your printer:* Unpack your printer according to the manufacturer's guide that came with the printer. You might need to install toner or ink, and also add paper. Then proceed to turn on your printer and ensure that it is not showing errors.

3. *Connect your printer:* Connect the printer over a network by using the guide that accompanied the printer.

   If you are using a Wi-Fi printer, there might be a need to connect your printer to the Mac using a USB cable in order to set up Wi-Fi printing. Once the printer has been connected safely to Mac, you can then install the Mac software that accompanied the printer, and connect your printer to the Wi-Fi network using the setup assistant of the printer. After successful setting up of the printer, you can detach your cable from the printer and Mac, while the printer will remain safely connected over the network.

4. *Add your printer to the list of available printers:* Click Apple menu , tap on

System Preferences, and then choose "Printers & Scanners."

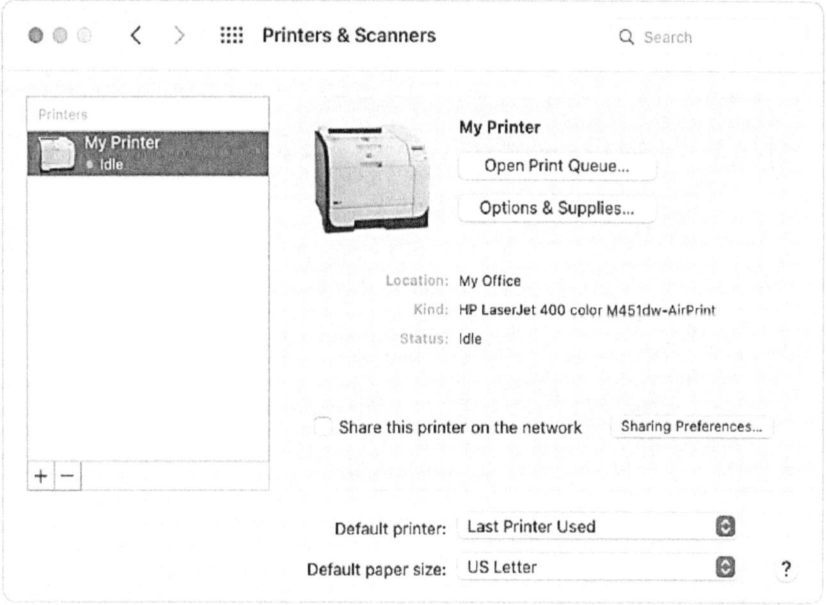

If you are unable to see your model of printer on the left where it should appear, tap on the Add button + found at the lower end of the list. You will get a dialogue with the list of printers available on your local network. Choose your printer when you see it on the list, and then click on "Add."

Add a Bluetooth printer to Mac

In case you have a Bluetooth enabled Mac or you have a USB Bluetooth adapter, you will be able to print files wirelessly to a printer that is Bluetooth-enabled.

5. *On Mac, update your software (in case you do not have an AirPrint printer):* Click on Apple menu, tap System Preferences, select Software Update, and then proceed to install any software that requires an update (list of software that needs to be updated will be provided). This step might be necessary even when Mac doesn't come up with any list to be updated, as it ensures that your Mac has the updated information about any printer software available from Apple. If you don't update software, you might be prompted with a message that the software is not available when you want to connect your printer to Mac. If your printer is AirPrint enabled, you do not have to check for any software update.

1. *Prepare your printer:* Unpack your printer according to the manufacturer's guide that came with the printer. You might need to install toner or ink, and also add paper. Then proceed to turn on your printer and ensure that it is not showing errors.
2. *Connect your printer:* Use the guide that accompanied your printer to get it ready to pair with Bluetooth.
3. *Add your Bluetooth printer to your list of printer:* Click on Apple menu, select "System Preferences," then select Printers & Scanners. Tap on the Add button +, and then click on the Default button.

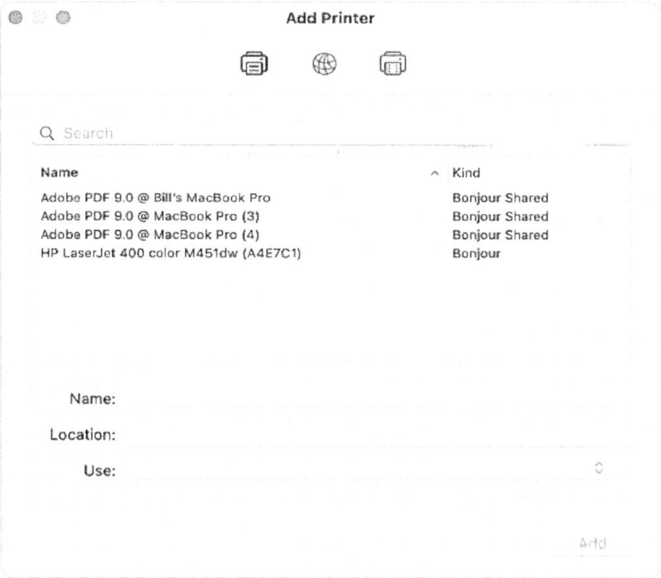

4. Choose your model of printer from the list of printers, and click on "Add." If you cannot see your own model of printer, you can enter the name inside the search bar and then tap "Return." If you cannot still see the name of your printer on the list, ensure that you are using the updated Bluetooth driver for the printer. You can check the manufacturer's website for the latest driver.

Once your printer has been connected successfully, and you receive a message asking you to download new software, kindly download and install the new software.

Organize your files in stacks on Mac

Use Stacks on Mac to organize your files and make them neat. Anytime you save or download a file on your Mac, it will be saved into the appropriate stack which helps to tidy your desktop.

Use stacks on the desktop

Stacks on Mac can be grouped or arranged by type (like PDFs or images), Finder tags, or date (like Date you last opened it or date you created it).

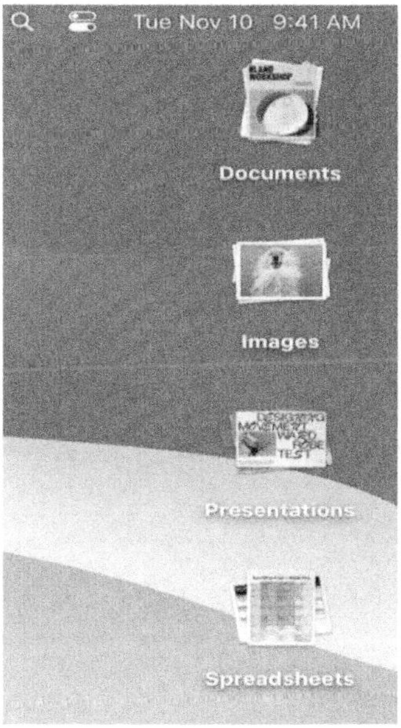

On your machine, carry out any of the actions below;

- *Turn on stacks:* Click on the desktop using the pointer, then click on View, and tap on "Use Stacks" or simply press Control-Command-0. Alternatively, control-click on the desktop and then select "Use Stacks."

- *Browse files in a stack:* Swipe to the left or to you right on the stack by using two fingers on your trackpad, but with one finger if you are using a magic mouse. You will be able to open a file that is at the top in a stack by tapping twice on such file.
- *Open or close a stack:* Click on the stack. Open a file by clicking twice on the file.
- *Change how stacks are grouped:* Use the pointer to click on the desktop, select View, click on "Group Stacks By," and then select an option, like Date Added. Or you can Control-click on the desktop, select "Group Stacks By," and then select an option.
- *Change how the stacks look:* Use the pointer to click on the desktop, select View, click on "Show View Options," and then change options. Alternatively, you can Control-click on the desktop, and then select Show View Options. From the options, you will be able to; make the icons look bigger, adjust (increase or reduce) the spacing between the icons,

display more info (like how files are in one stack), or move the icon labels to the side.

Use stacks in the Dock

From the Dock, you will have access to the **Downloads** stack where you can conveniently and quickly have access to the files you got from the web, accept with the AirDrop or received as an attachment (probably through mail).

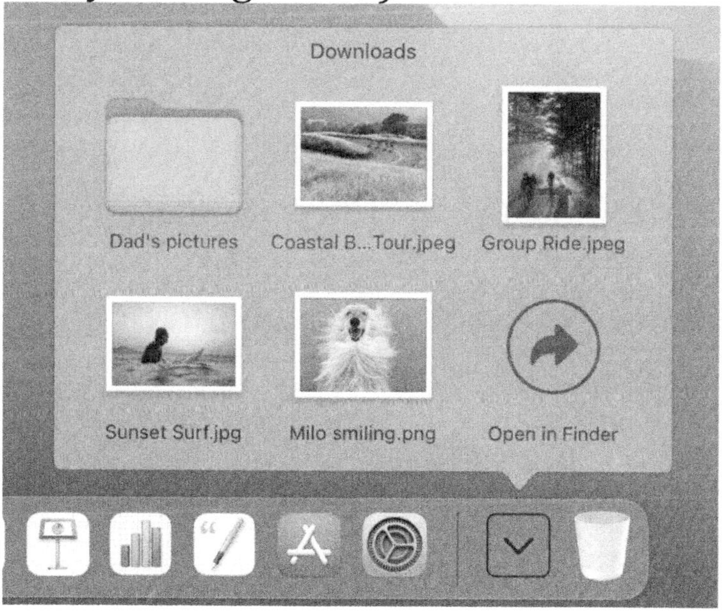

To aid quick accessibility, you will be able to add your folders and files to the Dock, and even show them as stack. An alias will be created by your Mac for the file or folder.

On your computer, carry out any of the actions below;

- *Add folders and files:* Drag and then drop a folder or file to the right side of the separator line (just after recently used apps).

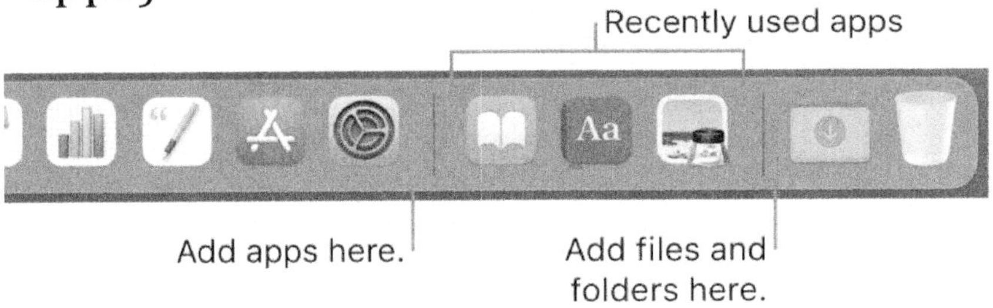

- *Open or close a file or folder:* Click on the folder or file. When the folder is opened, click twice on any item inside the folder to access it.
- *Change how folders appear:* Control-click your folder, and then indicate how you want the items inside the folder to be sorted, whether you plan to show the folder as a stack or in the Dock as a folder, and how to access the content of the folder (maybe in a fan or a grid).

CHAPTER FOUR

USING TOUCH ID ON Mac

If your own model of Mac comes with the Touch ID feature, then you will be able to use Touch ID to unlock your computer, validate purchases from the Apple Books, App Store and iTunes Store, and also do some purchases on the web with Apple Pay. Touch ID can also be used to sign into some of your downloaded third-party applications.

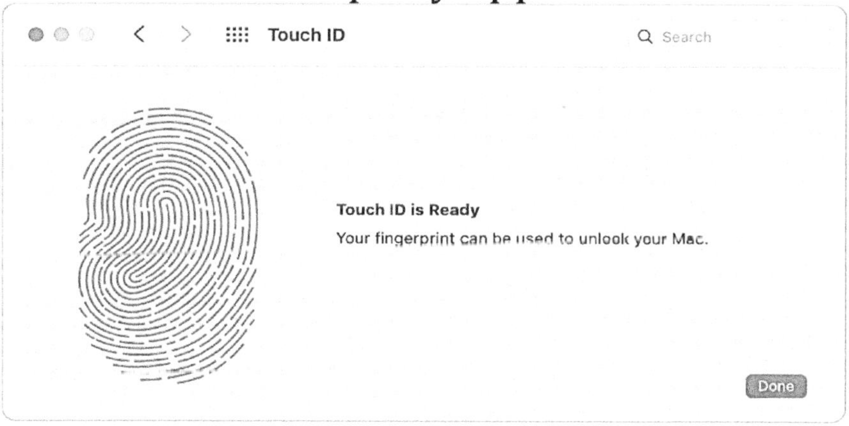

How to set up Touch ID feature on Mac

1. On your computer, click on Apple menu, select System Preferences, and then click on "Touch ID."

2. Choose "Add Fingerprint", input your password, and then proceed with the instructions on the screen. You will be able to add up to 3 fingerprints in your user account (you Mac, in total, can save up to 5 fingerprints).
3. Click on each of the following boxes to indicate how the Touch ID will be used by Mac;
   - *Unlocking your Mac:* Unlock Mac (after you must have wake Mac up from sleep) with the Touch ID.
   - *Apple Pay:* Complete any payment you make on Apple Pay with the Touch ID.
   - *iTunes Store, App Store & Apple Books:* Complete any payment you make on Apple online stores with the Touch ID.
   - *Password AutoFill:* Let the Touch ID automatically fill in credit card details, usernames and passwords when asked on Safari and some other platforms.

Rename or delete fingerprints

1. On your computer, click on Apple menu, select System Preferences, and then click on "Touch ID."
2. Carry out any of the actions below;
   - *Rename a fingerprint:* Tap the text just below a fingerprint, and then write a name.
   - *Delete a fingerprint:* Tap on a registered fingerprint, input your password, tap OK, and then select "Delete."

Use the Touch ID to unlock your Mac, log in or switch users

To deploy the Touch ID feature for these actions, you must have used password to log in to Mac already;

- *Unlock your Mac and some password-protected items:* Anytime you wake Mac up from sleep or open an app or item that is being protected by a password, just put your registered finger on Mac's Touch ID when requested. This will wake up the Mac or unlock the password-protected app or item as appropriate.

- *Log in to Mac from the login window:* Use the pointer to tap on your name from the login window, and then position your finger on the Touch ID. The Touch ID can only be used to unlock only the user accounts with passwords. You cannot use the Touch ID for guest accounts and share-only users' accounts.
- *Switch users for Mac:* Click on the user-switching menu from the Mac's menu bar, select another user, and then position your finger on the Touch ID.

If you want to be able to switch to a different user with the Touch ID, you must have set up the **fast user switching** option, and the user you want to switch to must have logged in to the Mac with a password in time past. To set up the fast user switching, see below;

Enable the fast user switching

1. On your computer, click on the Apple menu, select System Preferences, tap on "Users & Groups," and then click on "Login Options."

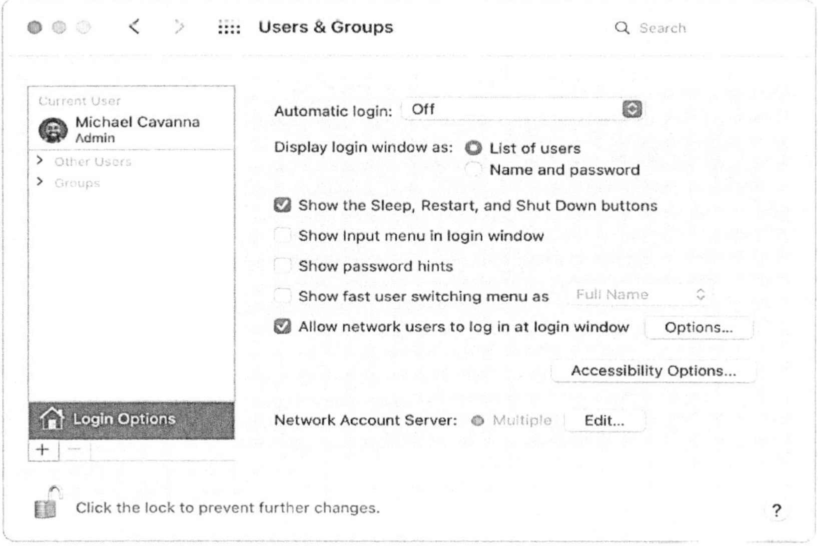

If you observe that the lock at the bottom left of the screen is locked, tap on the lock to unlock (access) the preference pane.

2. Choose the "Show fast user switching menu as", and then indicate how you want the fast user-switching menu to appear in your menu bar.

Purchase items with the Touch ID

1. Log in to Mac with your password.
2. Log in to one of the online stores or Apple Pay to buy items.
3. When requested, position your finger on the Mac's Touch ID to validate payment.

Having issues with the Touch ID?

- *Touch ID doesn't recognize fingerprints?* It is likely that your finger is dirty and wet, and that is why your Touch ID is unable to validate your finger. To get past this problem, make sure that your finger is dry and clean. Let your finger be free of lotion and moisturiser, as they hinder the working of the fingerprint recognition and make your finger difficult to read by the sensor.
- *If you still have to enter your password:* To enforce more security, you must enter your password on starting Mac. Sometimes, you will have to enter your pass-

word again to continue using the Touch ID. For instance, you must re-enter Mac's password every 2 days and after you must have entered the wrong password for five consecutive times.

Note: To enforce more securities, Touch ID details cannot be accessed by another user. This means that Touch ID information can only be seen by logged-in users, and the details cannot be modified by an administrator.

CHAPTER FOUR

USING APPS ON Mac

There are in-built apps that came pre-installed on your Mac, so that you can connect with friends (FaceTime), make calls (Contacts app), buy items (App Store) and do a lot of other things for free on your Mac. To access an app on your Mac, click on the app icon from the Dock (the Dock is found at the bottom of your screen), or tap on the Launchpad icon from your Dock, then open the app with Launchpad.

The following are apps that you can find pre-installed on your Mac;

App Store , Calculator app, Calendar app, Home app, Mail app, Messages, Maps, Music, Photos, Safari, TV, DVD Player, Image capture etc. There are lots of in-built apps on your Mac that you can lay your hands on, but this guide will only discuss the few important apps that you cannot do without.

The App Store

How to sign in to the Apple ID on Mac

The App Store on Mac is where you can explore and download important apps on your Mac. Nevertheless, before you will be able to do anything on the App Store, you will have to sign in to the App Store using your Apple ID.

1. From the App Store on Mac, tap "Sign In" found at the lower left corner of your screen.
2. Carry out any of these actions;
   - *Create an Apple ID (this is not necessary if you already have an Apple ID):* Click on "Create Apple ID," and then proceed with the instructions on the screen.

- *View account settings:* Tap on your name at the lower-left corner, and then click on "View Information."

  The account information that you will be able to view can include your billing information, Apple ID, and your nick-name (the one you use while reviewing apps). Hidden purchases can also be accessed.

View and manage purchased apps in the App Store on Mac

You will be able to see the list of apps that you have purchased (in the Purchased list) by using your Apple ID on any of your Macs. Also, you will be able to hide some apps that you don't want to see in the list, and install some apps that are no longer needed.

View purchased apps

- From the App Store on Mac, tap on your name from the lower-left corner or tap Sign In if you have not already signed in. Your account will be shown with all of the apps that you have purchased.

Hide and show apps

1. In the App Store on your Mac, click your name in the bottom-left corner or click Sign In if you're not already.
2. Carry out any of the actions below;
   - *Hide a purchased app:* Position your pointer over the app that you want to hide, click on the Show More button , and then select "Hide Purchase."
   - *View hidden apps:* Tap on "View Information." Click on "Managed" from the pop-up window, then tap "Unhide" found at the right side of the app that you want to show. When you are done, tap "Done."

Uninstall apps

- On Mac, drag the app that you want to uninstall from your Applications folder to the Trash (found at the end of your Dock), select Finder and then click on "Empty Trash."

Note: You will be unable to uninstall apps that are essential part of the macOS, like the mail app and the Safari browser.

Install purchases from the App Store on your Mac

There are more than one ways that you can use to install and reinstall apps you bought from the App Store with your Apple ID.

Note: In your App Store, your Apple ID is connected with all of the apps that you purchased with the ID, and you won't be able to transfer these apps to another Apple ID. In case you bought an app with your iPad, iPhone or another Mac computer, you should always endeavor to sign in with the same Apple ID so that you can see all of the apps you purchased on your Mac.

Install apps that you purchased on a different device

On other Macs, you will be able to install and also reinstall an app so far you purchased that app with your Apple ID.

- In the App Store on your Mac, click your name in the bottom-left corner or click Sign In if you are not already, then tap on the Download button.

Automatically download apps that you purchased on a different device

1. In the App Store on your Mac, click your name in the bottom-left corner or click Sign In if you are not already.
2. Tap App Store, select Preferences, and then choose "Automatically download apps purchased on other devices".

Reinstall apps

If you mistakenly or deliberately deleted or uninstalled a purchased app, you will be able to get it back by following the step below;

- In the App Store on your Mac, click your name in the bottom-left corner or click Sign In if you are not already, found the app that you want to reinstall, and then click on the Download button .

The Contacts App on Mac

Add contacts from iCloud, Google and more to Contacts on Mac

If you save your contacts in internet accounts — say for instance, Yahoo, Google or iCloud— the accounts can be used in your Contacts app, and you can view all your contacts in a single place.

Add a new account

1. From the Contacts app on Mac, click on Contacts, and then click on "Add Account."
2. Choose an account type or, if you are unable to see your type of account, click on "Other Contacts Account," and then tap Continue.

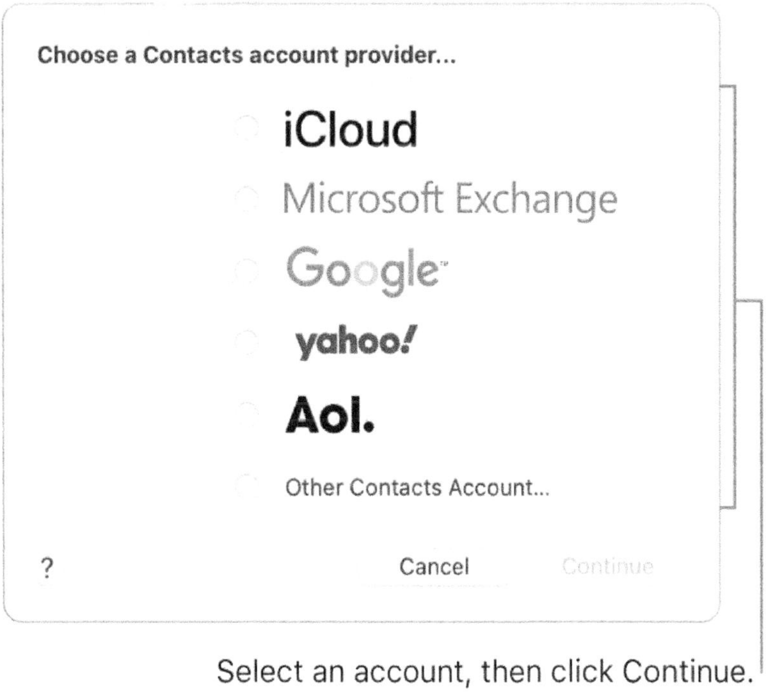

3. Input the information about your account.

   Ensure that the Contacts checkbox is marked for the account.

Add an account you already use on your Mac

1. From the Contacts app on Mac, click on Contacts, and then choose "Accounts to open Internet Accounts preferences."
2. Choose the account you plan to use from the left, and then select the Contacts box from the right.

Temporarily stop using an account

1. From the Contacts app on Mac, click on Contacts, and then choose "Accounts to open Internet Accounts preferences."
2. Choose the account from the left, and then unselect the Contacts box from the right.

To have access to the contacts again, enable the account by tapping on the account's tickbox.

Remove an account

1. From the Contacts app  on Mac, click on Contacts, select Preferences, and then tap on “”Accounts.
2. Choose an account, and then tap on the Remove button .

You can add the account back if you want to be seeing the contacts again.

Indicate your default Contacts account where contacts should be stored

If you have more than a single account in the Contacts app, new contacts will be automatically added to the account you have identified as the default Contacts account. To select your default Contacts account;

1. From the Contacts app  on Mac, click on Contacts, select Preferences, and then tap on “General.”
2. Tap on the Default Account pop-up menu (you will only see this if you have more than one Contacts accounts), and then

select the account that you want to use as default.

The FaceTime App on Mac

Sign in to FaceTime

You will be required to sign in to your FaceTime the very first time you launch the app, or when you signed out.

1. From the FaceTime app on Mac, input your Apple ID and password.
2. Tap "Next," and FaceTime will be "ON" automatically.

If you don't have an Apple ID, you will be able to create one from the Apple ID website.

Sign out of FaceTime

Note: Signing out of the FaceTime app will prevent you from receiving phone calls or FaceTime calls pending when you sign in to FaceTime again.

1. From the FaceTime app on Mac, click on FaceTime, select Preferences, and then click on "Settings."
2. Select "Sign Out."

Turn On/Off FaceTime

Turning off FaceTime will let you remain signed in to FaceTime but you won't be able to accept calls. If anyone calls you while you have turned off FaceTime, it will look (to the caller) as if you are not unavailable. Note that you won't get call notifications when you turn off FaceTime. To turn off or on FaceTime, follow the steps below;

Carry out any of the actions below with the FaceTime app on your Mac;

- *Turn off FaceTime:* Select FaceTime, and tap "**Turn FaceTime Off**."
- *Turn on FaceTime:* Select FaceTime, and tap "**Turn FaceTime On**."

Don't want to turn off FaceTime but want to stop FaceTime Notification from disturbing you?

If you don't want to disable FaceTime, but you don't want the FaceTime Notifications, simply enable the "Do Not Disturb" setting in the Control Center. This will prevent you from getting notifications you don't want.

Make calls in FaceTime on Mac

You will have to send a FaceTime call to one or many individuals using iPadOS, iOS or a macOS device.

Use Siri. Request something like:

- "FaceTime John"
- "FaceTime audio [*phone digit*]"

Enter the mail, phone number or name of the individual that you want to call in the search bar below, and then tap on **Audio** (to send audio call) or **Video** (to send video call).

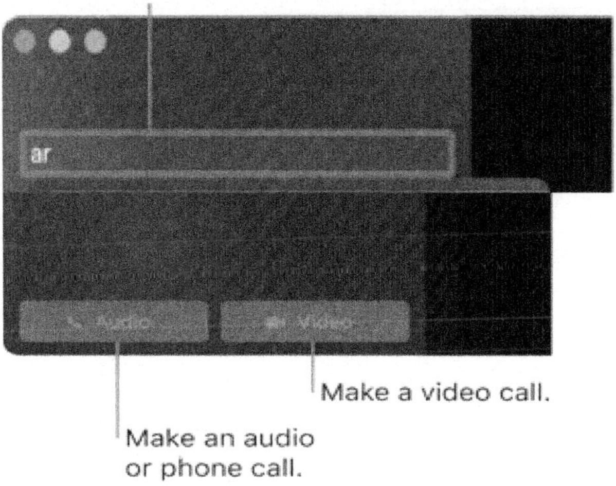

Make a FaceTime call

1. Launch the FaceTime app on Mac, and then sign in to your FaceTime account.
2. Inside the field at the top area of your FaceTime window, input the mail address or phone digit of the individual that you plan to send the call to, and then tap Return.
   Note: If you have been restricted to only call certain individuals, you will see an hourglass icon next to the persons you cannot call. This can occur probably when you have set up the limit for commu-

nications in Apple menu > System Preferences > Screen Time , and then tap **communication** from the sidebar of the screen time window. By tapping on **communications** from the sidebar, you will be able to restrict communication to certain groups of people. See the screenshot below;

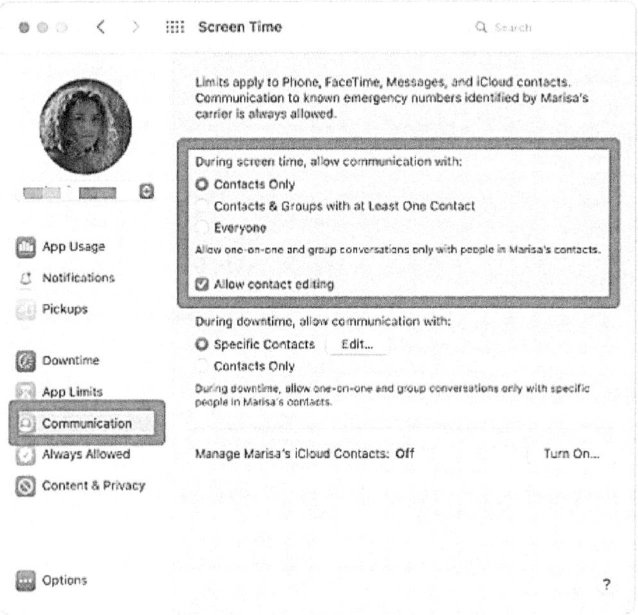

3. To initiate the FaceTime call, tap on the FaceTime

   Video button or click on the Audio button .

If you select the Audio button, you can decide whether you want to send a phone call or send a FaceTime audio call. The camera is turned off automatically while making a FaceTime audio call or a phone call.

4. While on a call, you will be able to; **pause the call, change the view of the call, mute the call or adjust the volume for the call,** and even **add more persons to your FaceTime call.**

If you send a video call and the receiver declined the call or the call was not answered, you can tap on the Message button to send an iMessage to the receiver. To send an iMessage, both you and the receiver must be signed in to iMessage.

Send a Group FaceTime call

With a Group FaceTime call, you will be able to send calls to about 32 persons at a time.

1. Launch the FaceTime app on Mac, and then sign in to your FaceTime account.

2. Inside the field at the top area of your FaceTime window, input the mail address or phone digit of the individual that you plan to send the call to, and then tap Return.

   Note: If you have been restricted to only call certain individuals, you will see an hourglass icon next to the persons you cannot call. This can occur probably when you have set up the limit for communications in Apple menu > System Preferences > Screen Time

   , and then tap **communication** from the sidebar of the screen time window. By tapping on **communications** from the sidebar, you will be able to restrict communication to certain groups of people.

3. Do step 2 again until you have all the members listed.

4. To initiate the FaceTime call, tap on the FaceTime Video button or click on the Audio button .

   If you select the Audio button , you can decide whether you want to send a phone call or send a FaceTime audio call. The camera is turned off automatically while making a FaceTime audio call or a phone call.

Each of the participants in a group FaceTime call will show in a tile on your screen. When any of the participants talks or you click on the tile, the tile will be displaced to the front and will then become very prominent. Some of the tiles that will not be able to fit exactly on your screen will rather appear in a row located at the bottom. If there are any of the participants you cannot see, you can swipe through the rows to find him or her.

How to pause a FaceTime video call

On your machine, perform any of the actions below while making a video call;

- *Pause a video call:* From your FaceTime app , tap on the yellow minimize icon located at the top section of your FaceTime window or you can quickly switch to a different app to pause FaceTime video call.

  Note: During a Group video call, the yellow minimize icon will only minimize your screen but won't pause the video call.

- *Resume a paused video call:* Tap on your FaceTime app icon from the Dock.

End a call

Launch your FaceTime app on Mac, and carry out one of these actions to terminate FaceTime call;

- *End an audio call:* Tap on the "End button " from the notification.

- *End a video call:* Hover your pointer over the call window, and then select the End Call button .

Terminating a FaceTime Group call from your end doesn't necessarily end the call for other members in the group. That said, a Group FaceTime call will still be active until all the members lcave the Group call. You can rejoin the Group call by clicking on the "Join Video button ."

The Home App

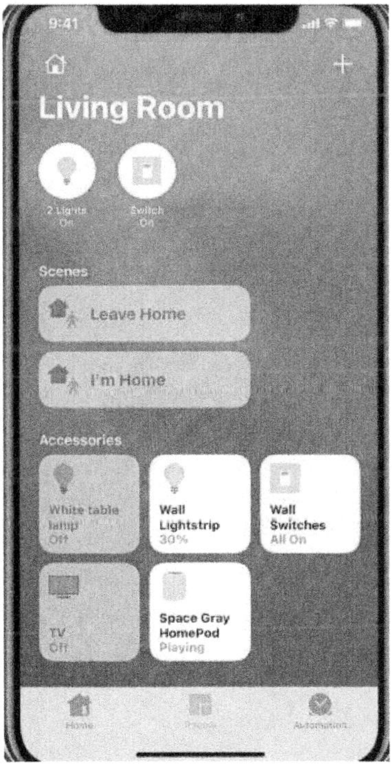

Automate HomeKit-enabled accessories, like smart plugs, smart TVs, Cameras, locks, thermostats, lights etc by using the Home app to give you a secure means of controlling these accessories all in a single click. You will also be able to group multiple speakers to start playing the same audio, receive a notification when a doorbell camera supported by the Home App identifies a visitor at your doorstep, access and record videos from a supported security camera. With the Home feature, you can use the Apple HomeKit accessory to control any assignment on your iPhone.

You can leverage on the Apple Home app to control Apple-enabled Home tools in your house even when you are not at home. With your Home app, you can control lighting, locks to your room or house, Apple TV, cameras, etc.

How to add Home accessories on your Mac

You will not be able to add accessories to Home with your Mac, as only an iPhone, iPad or iPod touch can be used to add accessories to Home.

To add a HomeKit accessory to the Home app on iPhone, you will need to make sure that the accessory is powered on and that it is nearby. In addition, you will need to check the manual for the accessory to confirm whether it requires some extra hardware to work with HomeKit. To add an accessory to Home on iPhone, follow the steps below;

- Select the Home tab, and then tap.
- Click on "Add Accessory," and then proceed with the instructions displayed on the screen.

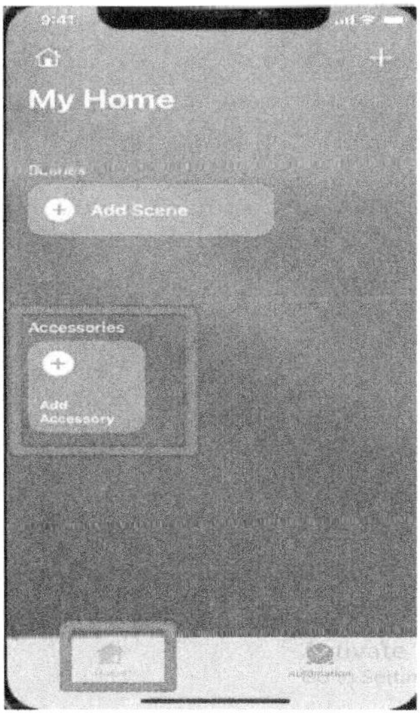

- Any added accessory to Home is assigned autom-atically to a default room on your Home App or any room you selected.
- You will be requested to use your device's camera to scan the QR code or to input the 8-digit setup code embedded on the accessory. To check the accessory's QR code, check the box or the manual that came with the accessory. You will then be required to join the accessory to a room in your iPhone's Home app. You can give the room a specific name that you will be using to control the accessory with "Hello Siri."

Note: Although you won't be able to add Home accessories on Mac, because adding them on your iPhone or iPad will make those Home accessories appear on Mac once you have signed in with the same Apple ID and password (on both your Mac and iPhone).

Control an accessory on Mac

- From the Home app on Mac, select an accessory to turn on/off the accessory.

Double-click on the accessory to access more options. The type of accessory will determine the available controls for the accessory. For instance, some light bulbs will allow you to change brightness and colors.

CHAPTER FIVE

THE APPLE ID AND PASSWORD

Create an Apple ID on Mac

With your Apple ID on Mac, you will have access to the App Store, iCloud, Apple Books, FaceTime, iTunes Store and most other Apple services. Apple ID consists of your current email address and a password. It is advisable that you used the same Apple ID and password across all of your Apple devices. For instance, if you have a Mac, iPhone, iPad and an iPod touch, you should try to use the same Apple ID across these devices for seamless transactions.

You can use your active email address to create your Apple ID or use the @icloud mail address that will be automatically generated for you when you want to register.

You can either log in to Apple ID account website at https://appleid.apple.com/uk to create your Apple identity or create your own Apple ID on your Mac, iOS or iPadOS device.

In some countries, you will be able to use your phone number instead of your mail address as the Apple ID.

Read the instruction below to create your Apple ID with your active mail address or the iCloud address that will be generated for you;

1. On your computer, select Apple menu, tap on System Preferences, and then choose "Sign In."
2. Scroll down a bit and click on "Create Apple ID," and then proceed with the instructions that will be provided for you on the screen.

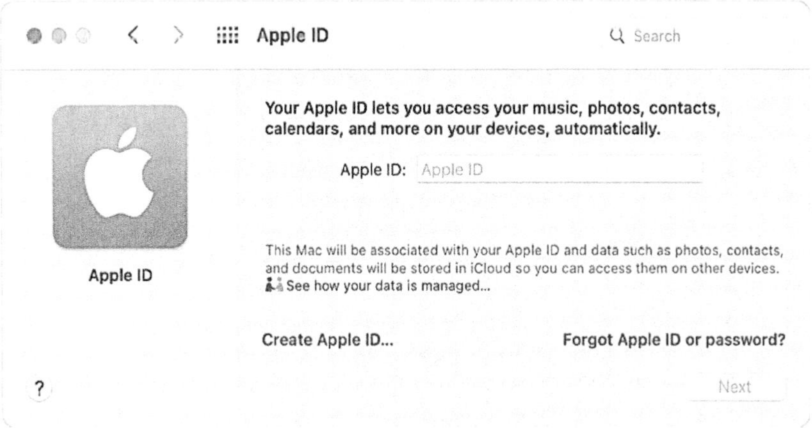

Set up your Apple ID payment method and shipping address on Mac

You can modify the payment and shipping details linked with your Apple ID by using the "Payment & Shipping preferences." To do this;

1. On Mac, click on Apple menu, tap System Preferences, tap Apple ID, and then click on Payment & Shipping from the sidebar menu.

   If you are yet to sign in to your Apple ID, tap "Sign In," enter your Apple ID details and follow the instructions on the screen.

2. You can change the details below;

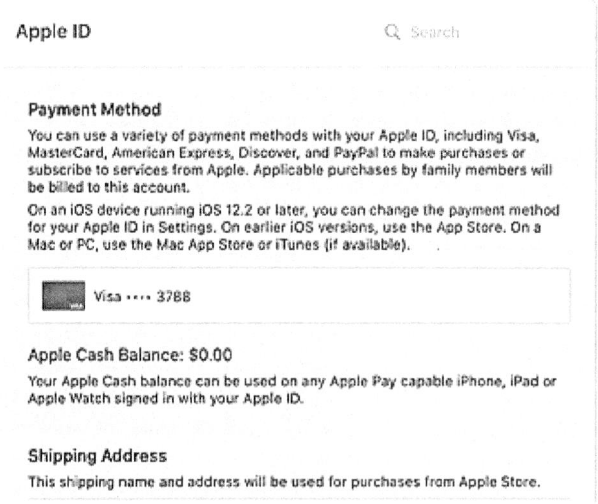

- *Payment Method:* There are many payment methods available for your Apple ID, which include PayPal, Visa, MasterCard, American Express etc which can be used to validate purchases from Apple platforms. The payment method can be changed by clicking on "Details" and then input your billing address and credit card details.
- *Apple Cash Balance:* Shows your Cash Balance. This balance can be used on any iPhone, Apple Watch or iPad signed in with your Apple ID.
- *Shipping Address:* Displays the name and the shipping address you are using to validate purchases on Apple Store. Tap "Add a shipping address" to input your postal address. Tap "Edit" if you wish to modify your shipping address.

Customize the desktop picture on your Mac

Decide on the picture you want to use as your desktop display. This is the picture that will appear at the background on your desktop, and you can always change it anytime you want. Mac comes with many desktop pictures you can select from, and you can also use your own customized pictures or colors as the desktop background.

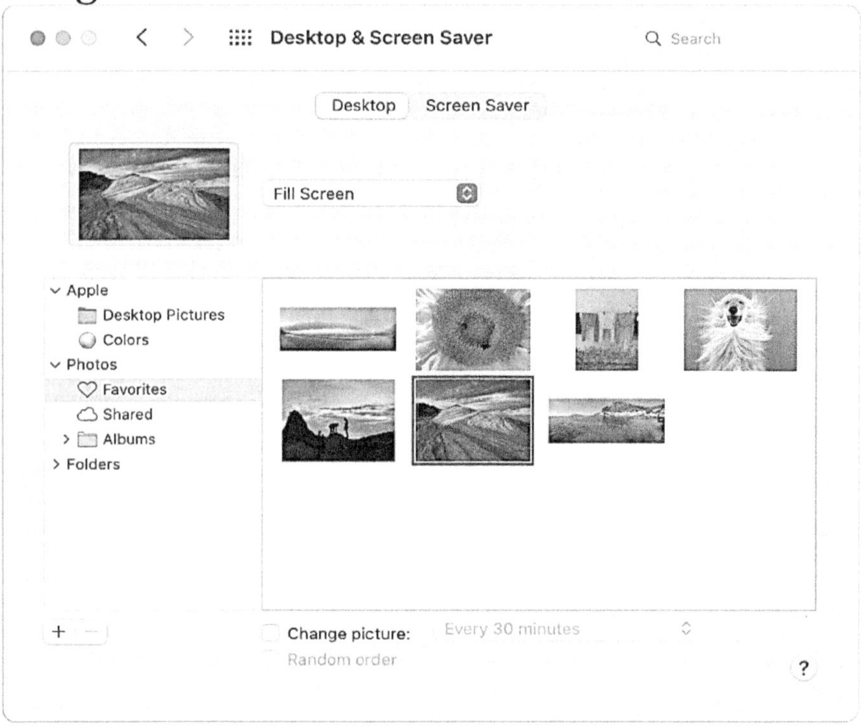

1. On Mac, click on the Apple menu, select System Preferences, choose Desktop & Screen Saver, and then click on "Desktop."
2. From the left pane, select a color or picture:
   - *Pictures and colors that come default with your Mac:* Tap on the arrow beside Apple (look at the screenshot above), then choose a folder, like Colors or Desktop Pictures, to avail yourself with the thumbnails of available colors or pictures.
   - *Your pictures:* Click on the arrow beside Photos (or iPhoto as it might be applicable). If the picture you want to use is inside another folder or in the Pictures, tap on the arrow beside Folders, and then choose a folder.

     Click on the Add button to add folder, scroll to the folder and select it, then click on "Choose."

2. From the right pane, select the picture that you plan to use.

   The desktop will change immediately, so that you will be able to preview how the picture looks for the desktop. When you are using your own picture as the desktop background, you can make it fill the whole screen, let it be at the center or arrange it as you deem fit.

About Author

Robert Kissinger is an Apple developer with five years of experience coding Apple apps. He also takes active interest in reviewing gadgets and software. He has written several user guides on iOS, iPadOS, Apple Watch and macOS.

Robert studied computer science and Engineering from the University of Michigan, USA.

Printed in Great Britain
by Amazon

54452326R00098